WHAT OTHERS HAD TO SAY...

"Mrs. Smith wrote from her heart and experiences, transcending me the reader, to where she was in Afghanistan! Being a preacher of the gospel, I plan to utilize Mrs. Smith's 'teachable moments' into also 'preachable moments' on Sunday mornings!"

— Dr. Daniel L. Russell, Jr., Senior Pastor, New Life Deliverance Temple

"Florence Robyn Smith profoundly shares 179 teachable moments during her deployment to Afghanistan. This book is full of practical wisdom and spiritual insights. She takes simple and, at times, traumatic experiences and extracts 'life lessons' from them. She has done a masterful job of showing her readers that there is a lesson to be learned from all that we experience in life. Instead of complaining about our situations, we need to learn from them and search God's Word for scriptures to support the lesson. I loved this book!"

— Mrs. Lisa P. Lewis, Vice President/Administrative Director, Seeds of Greatness Ministries/Seeds of Greatness Bible Church

"What an amazing journey... I just completed *Afghanistan: 179 Days of Teachable Moments*, and so appreciated the invitation Florence 'Robyn' Smith offered to share her the ups and downs of being deployed in Afghanistan from February until August in 2012. In 2 Corinthians 3:2, the Apostle Paul spoke of his followers being 'epistles' known and read of all men. That verse ran so true as I read each account and experience that God was sharing with 'Robyn' and her wonderful way of finding Spirit-led insights from scripture, along with down home, sometime motherly, words of wisdom for future travelers in life.

Each day, 'Robyn' took what might have seemed like random acts from sitting in the sun to her seat assignment on a plane to share God's handiwork, His love for us His children, and our need to be obedient to His commands. From zippers being like the Body of Christ to the analogy of workers shoveling dirt and our need to dig deep to 'root out sin in our lives', she like a chef provided daily rations to carry us along our God ordained steps without falling. I'm so proud of my big sister for accepting this assignment and very grateful that she wanted to share what she learned with us.

While few of us will have to travel 7,000 miles or be deployed by the U.S. Government in a hostile war zone, 'Robyn's' faith, courage, and commitment to obey God should send a powerful message to us all about taking up our crosses daily and following Him. *Afghanistan: 179 Days of Teachable Moments*, I salute you my sister and co-laborer in God's army."

— Elder George W. Hawkins Jr., Pastor, High Calling
Ministries

AFGHANISTAN:

179 DAYS OF

TEACHABLE MOMENTS

AFGHANISTAN:

179 DAYS OF

TEACHABLE MOMENTS

FLORENCE ROBYN SMITH

TEACHABLE MOMENTS
PRESS
Elkridge, Maryland

All Scripture quotations are taken from the King James Version of the
Holy Bible.

─────────────

AFGHANISTAN: 179 Days of Teachable Moments

─────────────

ISBN-13: 978-0-9905811-0-9
ISBN-10: 0990581101
Printed in the United States of America

TEACHABLE MOMENTS
PRESS
Teachable Moments Press
6030 Marshalee Drive, #175
Elkridge, MD 21075
www.teachablemomentspress.com

─────────────

Library of Congress Control Number: 2014914451

─────────────

DISCLAIMER STATEMENT

The views expressed in this book are the personal ones of the author and do not reflect the official policy or position of the U.S. Government, the Department of Defense, or any of its components.

DEDICATION

I wish to thank God for the opportunity afforded to me to complete the deployment and publish this inspiring work. To the memory of my dear mother, Rita Sara Robinson Smith, who was the ultimate inspiration for her children in sharing her gifts of music, writing and drama.

I could not have completed this project without the love and support of my dear husband, Francis; my children: Christina and her husband Calvin and their two boys, Isaiah and Titus and daughter Lauren; my middle child, Francis, Jr. (T.J.); and Kamille and her husband James and their son, Jayson and daughter London. In addition, I am grateful for the prayers of my entire family, especially my brother Billy whose heart ached for my safety.

Finally, I dedicate this book to my precious father, Marion O. Smith, Sr., whom I love and only wanted to make him proud of my journey and accomplishments. I survived on my prayer and desire for God to keep him with us until my return… *"for he is faithful that promised"* (Hebrews 10:23).

CONTENTS

ACKNOWLEDGMENTS

I appreciate the love demonstrated by the people of God who emptied their hearts out in prayer for my safety. For your diligent prayers, I want to thank all members and friends of the Gospel Spreading Church of God.

The encouragement from my Department of Defense mentor, Mr. Thomas N. Tomaszewski and my special co-workers gave me the enthusiasm to finish the manuscript.

A sincere thanks and appreciation goes to all who assisted with the writing, editing, review, marketing and publication of this work. Special recognition to:

Editors—Jan Sherman and Timothy Sherman, Between the Lines, LLC

Book Cover Design and Marketing Materials—Calvin E. Robertson, Jr., Eve of Creativity

Author Photograph and Trailer—James C. Daniels, III, Don't Judge Me Productions

Promotions—Ruth G. Robinson, Adjunct Professor, Hampton University

Social Media Manager—Pauline S. Cook, Local Business Cons

Dr. Almeta Stokes—for writing the Preface, Tallit guidance, and your fervent prayers.

Mrs. Lisa P. Lewis—for your sincere review of the manuscript and engrafting my children and family into the Seeds Family.

Dr. Daniel L. Russell, Jr.—for your candid and detailed review of the manuscript—you were definitely a life-saver.

Elder George W. Hawkins, Jr.—for esteeming me to the level of one of your sisters and taking the time to provide your review.

Ms. Rhonda L. Smith—for your willingness to assist me with this project.

I am grateful to everyone who has poured into my spiritual development and work life. I thank God and you for the honor of sharing these teachable moments with you.

PREFACE

I am honored to have been invited to write the Preface for *Afghanistan: 179 Days of Teachable Moments*. This book delves into many private moments in the life of one who lived for six months in a war zone.

As I read the text, I was engrossed and intrigued. I found it hard to pull away. I read the manuscript journal during several trips by auto and by air.

There are two poignant factors that are embedded in my mind from the reading. First, the learning gained from reading this book was incredible. The military life I saw was raw and straightforward. My deepest emotions were stirred as I read page after page.

I thought about the fact that as executive officer, Florence "Robyn" Smith's tasks and responsibilities included duties such as nighttime charge officer and supervisor of individuals whose culture suggested that men, rather than women typically assume positions of authority. I am sure these conditions weighed heavily on "Robyn" physically as well as psychologically. Indeed, I learned of the extreme danger and high risks to which our military personnel are subjected on a regular basis.

Secondly, I was struck by "Robyn's" strong belief in and reliance upon God for protection and safety during her deployment. I wondered what happens when nonbelievers are placed in similar situations without God or His Son to lean upon. Whence comes strength in times of intense fear?

Throughout the manuscript I noticed that "Robyn" referenced Scripture verses and personal prayers that brought encouragement and hope in times of threat, especially during Ramadan season. An example of complete faith in God was "Robyn's" determination to head home from Afghanistan on August 13, 2012 in spite of the announcement that all should avoid travel on that day. Her trust in Jehovah is so strong and vibrant that she told her Commander that God would see her through just as He had done for six months, and He did.

I am pleased to have had the opportunity to read about life on the military compound. I vicariously witnessed the sights, sounds and fears of a combat zone. I am thrilled that "Robyn's" tenure was only six months. I wonder how folk with longer deployments fare psychologically.

This journal, interspersed with words of deliverance and victory, expresses the reality of Psalm 91, Psalm 23, and Joshua 1:9. This book is strongly recommended for persons desiring spiritual growth and those pursuing military careers or civil service.

— Dr. Almeta Stokes, Professor, Howard University

INTRODUCTION

This book is a collection of inspirational nuggets through which God taught me about His nature and how my personal life experiences related to His Word. These personal events occurred during my six-month deployment to Kabul, Afghanistan, February 14 – August 16, 2012 and had a profound impact on my spiritual growth.

As I have shared some of these experiences with others, they have encouraged me that these teachable moments are not just mine alone. These friends, family and co-workers have also benefited from my journal of experiences. Tears were shed and laughter spilled over as people grabbed hold of the universal truths and made them their own. So, in response to their urgings, I decided to share my diary of teachable moments with the world.

The following scripture is the foundation as to why I penned this volume. *"Shew me thy ways, O Lord; teach me thy paths. Lead me in thy truth, and teach me: for thou art the God of my salvation; on thee do I wait all the day"* (Psalms 25:4-5).

Teachable moments were not new to me. Prior to my deployment, teachable moments were integrated into my Bible study topics taught during the Youth and Young Adult Bible Study at the Church of God in Baltimore, Maryland. But these simple, practical, life-application moments that arose in Afghanistan brought me to yield to the Holy Spirit at an entirely new level.

My desire is that each reader will learn something from these teachable moments and subsequently draw closer to God.

Throughout my deployment, I found life lessons rising from the smallest of events. I hope readers will be able to find the voice of God in the little moments of each day and grow as I did. Ultimately, my desire is that readers will be given new insight with a sharpened spiritual perception.

The decision to deploy to a combat zone was not a hasty one. It took me three years to get to the point to discuss it with my husband, Francis. I went to God, asking for direction and confirmation. He gave me: *"For I know the thoughts that I think toward you, saith the Lord, thoughts of peace, and not of evil, to give you an expected end"* (Jeremiah 29:11).

I was humbled and honored to be part of a team of professionals assigned to one of the nation's most sensitive missions in Afghanistan. I invite you to share in my journey as I reveal how a 53-year-old grandmother (sporting two weapons, 35 pounds of individual body armor, combat boots and a helmet) completed her mission as Executive Officer (XO) for a Compound located in Kabul, Afghanistan: a city filled with threat tributaries flowing toward an ambiguous future.

FEBRUARY 2012

14 February ~ "Departure Day"

The children and grandchildren came to town to celebrate my departure and see me off at the airport. My middle child, T.J., could not bear to see me leave, so he didn't accompany me to the airport. It was my husband, Frank; daughters: Christina and Kamille; and grandchildren: Isaiah, Titus and Jayson whose faces showed their support and love in the waiting area.

The night before I left, we were up late packing last-minute items and the family shared some parting gifts. The kids bought me a mini iPod onto which T.J. loaded all my iTunes albums. I didn't know that the children grabbed the journal I had packed to jot down my experiences, and each wrote parting words of encouragement for me to read later. These are their farewell wishes:

From Kamille:
Mommy, I am so proud of you and the adventure you are about to embark upon. You have always told us to go for what we want and you did just that. You are a blessed woman of God and the blood of Jesus will cover you to and from. May God show you great things while you are away. You are going to come back even more powerful than you are now. I love you, I'll miss you, but I am grateful that God is giving you the chance to go on this journey.— sga de zer lido pe nita (see you soon)!

From Christina:

This must be how Peter felt as he threw one foot over the side of the boat (See Matthew 14:24-34). There were people urging him not to, but a greater calling was pulling him in.

The environmental conditions were less than desirable, but peace made his path so clear that the surroundings were no longer visible. All that Peter knew of and was sure of no longer existed as he stepped into the water. The physical laws on the earth gave way to the spiritual laws of the Father and off he went into the *extraordinary*.

This is where He desires that we venture into the *extraordinary*. There He is with you and only asks that you keep your eyes on Him because, as you venture out, nothing will be familiar—the waters are uncharted. But how does one know how to navigate in the *extraordinary* unless someone who has been there already teaches them?

We patiently await your return home so that you can teach us how to walk in the *extraordinary*.

From T.J.

So it's hard to find words to tell you just how much you mean to me, and my mind goes blank finding a way to say bye. I know it'll only be six months, but I am sad you won't be here to have those afternoon chats about what's going on at work or what those crazy Republicans are up to. Just promise me that you won't worry too much about me and Dad. We got this! We'll be good. Don't let anyone stress you out over there, and remember we love you and support all that you're doing for our country. Can't wait till you get back. Love, T.J.

Humbly, I read these words and knew that the joining of their faith to mine would make an incredible difference on this dangerous, but important, journey. The love of family is like none other. I can't imagine those who are deployed without the support from home. The incomparable love of my family gave me strength, willpower, courage and the tenacity to succeed with this mission.

"Nay, in all these things we are more than conquerors through him that loved us. For I am persuaded, that neither death, nor life, nor angels, nor principalities, nor powers, nor things present, nor things to come, Nor height,

nor depth, nor any other creature, shall be able to separate us from the love of God, which is in Christ Jesus our Lord" (Romans 8:37-39).

14 February ~ "The Broken Zipper"

I received a going away gift from a special young couple, Darryl and Kim McIntosh. It was a small, over-the-shoulder military satchel. I really loved this backpack. Somehow I managed to dislodge the zipper, which made it useless. As if this was not exacerbating enough, I had it stuffed with items I needed while in flight. I was determined to fix it before I left, but to no avail. However, my girls Christina and Kamille each put their efforts into fixing it. We looked up the term **"broken zipper"** on the Internet to find a solution and "Miss Fix-it Christina" was successful! She not only fixed the zipper, but also sewed extra reinforcement at the end to keep it from separating again. This led to the first "teachable moment" of my deployment.

I thought about how the teeth of the zipper must come together in a certain way in order for it to stay together and perform its intended function. When people in the Body of Christ are joined together as a zipper, the connection creates such a bond that we keep in what's good and keep out what's not good or needed. When that zipper is broken, it creates havoc. Just one faulty tooth in a zipper can cause the entire product to be ruined.

I learned the lesson that each one of us is needed to keep this Body of Christ together for the edification of the whole. Some of us may think we aren't that important. In fact, we might think we wouldn't be noticed if we disappeared. Yet, God has designed us to be linked perfectly together. Even one person missing or out of place can wreak havoc on the Church's mission. I thought about the following scripture verses:

"For as the body is one, and hath many members, and all the members of that one body, being many, are one body: so also is Christ … For the body is

not one member, but many. If the foot shall say, Because I am not the hand, I am not of the body; is it therefore not of the body? And if the ear shall say, Because I am not the eye, I am not of the body; is it therefore not of the body? If the whole body were an eye, where were the hearing? If the whole were hearing, where were the smelling? But now hath God set the members every one of them in the body, as it hath pleased him. And if they were all one member, where were the body? But now are they many members, yet but one body. Now ye are the Body of Christ, and members in particular" (1 Corinthians 12:12, 14-20, 27).

15 February ~ "Let Your Light Shine"

I am looking out the window of the plane over East Asia and my eyes are drawn upward. Either we are closer to them in this part of the earth or it's because we're flying so high in the heavens, but the stars are so vivid—they look like you can reach out and touch them. There are big ones, little ones, bright ones, and dim ones. Nonetheless, they are all shining. It is truly inspiring.

Scripture refers to the righteous people of God as stars in Daniel 12:3. You are a star! No matter what your state, size, position, level, proportion—SHINE! What you do in your little corner of humanity does matter. As the sky is littered with stars, this world is inundated with His people. Do your part, little or great, to let the world know there is a Savior. Be a light to this dying world, which stumbles in the darkness of sin. SHINE!

"And they that be wise shall shine as the brightness of the firmament; and they that turn many to righteousness as the stars for ever and ever" (Daniel 12:3).

16 February ~ "Use What's Available"

This was such a draining journey. I had to maneuver in and out of customs, dragging my heavy bags around, waiting for my flight to Bagram, only to find out that we had to make a stop in Kuwait to pick up a company of soldiers. I flew on the C-130 aircraft with cumbersome individual body armor (IBA) and the temperature on the plane was freezing cold! When we stopped in Kuwait, I gobbled down chow-hall fries, cornbread and a plum. I had an urgent need to go to the bathroom, but there were only outside porta potties…yuck!

Well, sometimes you have to **use what's available** even though it seems primitive. There are times that we need to experience the plight of others to learn to be thankful for the abundance and pleasures of life. My thoughts were: "I'm perplexed right now, but will **use what's available**. I'm upset right now about using the porta potty, but after realizing that the situation could be worse, I'll **use what's available**." God tells us that He can use the simple to confuse the wise. So I am in good company. Let this "wise" one learn how to be grateful for the facility in front of her!

"But God hath chosen the foolish things of the world to confound the wise; and God hath chosen the weak things of the world to confound the things which are mighty;" (1 Corinthians 1:27).

16 February ~ "Use Your Gear for Comfort"

Our flight to Bagram was definitely uncomfortable. I observed the 120+ soldiers around me sleep as best they could with their gear of weapons and helmets packed tightly and neatly. Many used their gear as a pillow, some hugged their gear for support, and others rested their bodies on their gear. Their seating was very tight, shoulder to shoulder. Some were tall, short, small, big…no one complained—they all were tired.

My crew sat in the jump seats with no arm rests or padding. Suddenly, I thought to myself, "What did I do with my helmet? I hope it's under my seat somewhere."

I popped a Listerine tablet in my mouth, thanks to Mary Haines' great travel gift! In fact all gifts given were very useful for my trip. God sure knows how to use people to bless others with gifts of comfort for austere times. Wow God, You are really teaching me and it's only Day 3 of the trip. So, I'll use what I have and get as comfortable as possible for the remaining flight.

I'm learning to adapt to events and situations outside my "normal." Paul said, *"I know how to be abased and to abound, in all, be content"* (Philippians 4:12). There's no room for claustrophobia in contentment!

"I know both how to be abased, and I know how to abound: every where and in all things I am instructed both to be full and to be hungry, both to abound and to suffer need" (Philippians 4:12).

17 February ~ "I Will Trust When I Cannot See"

While on the flight to Kabul, the clouds were so thick that we couldn't see a thing! Thankfully, the pilots have instruments to guide them when they cannot see. I would have hated to have us fly into something! Actually, these instruments are more trustworthy than visual cues. A pilot may see the zenith or horizon and become confused as to whether they are flying upside down or upright.

We must trust God when we cannot see our way through a problem or trial. The instruments given to us—the Holy Spirit, prayer, trust, and confidence—these are better guides than our own insight. These instruments will help steer us through the darkest and thickest clouds of trial to the ultimate path God has set for us. We should trust and be patient, knowing that we will reach our destination. We came through the clouds and landed safely in the snowy weather.

"Behold, God is my salvation; I will trust, and not be afraid: for the LORD JEHOVAH is my strength and my song; he also is become my salvation" (Isaiah 12:2).

18 February ~ "The Accurate Inventory"

I spent most of my first work day with the departing Executive Officer (XO) and our Senior Logistician working on the inventory reconciliation. If a serial number was not identified with an item, we had an issue. But if we had an item not listed on the inventory sheet, then it was a freebie—it belonged to no one. We inventoried $4.5M of equipment for our unit. Letters and numbers were in my dreams that night!

We are the items and the Book of Life is the inventory sheet. We are ensured that our names are written in the Book of Life when we receive salvation. God knows those that are His. We should live our lives so that we are accounted for by Jesus on that great judgment day. Stay on the list!

"Notwithstanding in this rejoice not, that the spirits are subject unto you; but rather rejoice, because your names are written in heaven" (Luke 10:20).

19 February ~ "Surviving the Power of Mother Nature"

It is really cold here. I put on a hat, gloves, jacket, thick socks, and boots, yet I could stand to be outside only for a little while. When I realized that the protection I had was no match for Mother Nature, I chose to retreat inside where it was dry and warm. Good choice! We must prepare ourselves with protection to withstand **the power of Mother Nature**. God may send cold days but we must be wise to understand our human limits while encountering the elements.

We ought to be wise and know our limits in certain situations and make intelligent decisions. God has given us good sense and intelligence—we need to use it! As I was in prayer tonight, God reminded me how He would guide and direct my steps. By His lead, I can exercise the wisdom that I need to more than survive.

"Wisdom is the principal thing; therefore get wisdom: and with all thy getting get understanding" (Proverbs 4:7).

20 February ~ "Just For Me"

It snowed most of the day today. I was told that Afghanistan had received an unusual amount of snowfall this year. As I looked up at the flakes floating down from the sky, all I could say was, "Thank You Lord!" God sent the snow to Earth to cleanse the environment **JUST FOR ME!** Snow can purify and improve the air quality, which is needed here in Afghanistan.

I've been claiming great health all week—I have declared healing and no feeling of sickness over my life. I am in God's care to stay healthy. First of all, I receive three meals a day; now isn't God good? And next, God is sending all this snow as part of His plan to keep me healthy!

"He giveth snow like wool: he scattereth the hoarfrost like ashes" (Psalms 147:16).

20 February ~ "The Bumps in the Road"

While driving through the city today, we often hit potholes that rocked the car back and forth. Some holes were filled with objects in an attempt to lessen the hole, but create a bumpy ride. The snow, ice and wet conditions made it worse. Driving around the potholes is mostly impossible due to surrounding obstacles. When there is no place to go, we were forced to drive through the potholes. But this doesn't stop anyone from their activities. Everyone continues to go about their travels; vehicles, animals and bicycles, all rocking and swaying as they maneuvered through the potholes.

Even though there may be **bumps in the road**, we can still make it to our destination. We ought to ride over each one with care and keep moving. If we stop, we might get stuck in the mire of negative circumstances. These bumps are just that—bumps; they do not define us or our destination. They are just part of the path we take. We must stay focused and not let the things of this world distract us so that we refuse to move forward as we travel this road to Heaven.

"Set your affection on things above, not on things on the earth" (Colossians 3:2).

21 February ~ "Sweep the Dust, Not Only the Dirt"

Today while sweeping the conference room and the XO/1SGT office spaces, I noticed a lot of dust that had been left under the bench. Sometimes we are good about getting the dirt, but seem to miss the dust! Why, because feather-weight particles are harder to detect.

In our walk with God, we can often easily call out those visible dirty sins, but fail to address the dust in our hearts—also known as secret or subtle sins. When we perform a good house cleaning of our hearts, we must make sure we get the dust also. The dust will eventually become dirt when it has been left there too long. We need to seek God for the purging of our hearts. His cleaning agent of the Holy Spirit can clean away every speck. **Sweep the Dust as well as the Dirt**!

"I acknowledge my sin unto thee, and mine iniquity have I not hid. I said, I will confess my transgressions unto the LORD; and thou forgavest the iniquity of my sin. Selah" (Psalms 32:5).

22 February ~ "Speak to My Heart Holy Spirit"

There were riots in Bagram yesterday and we are still on lock down today. The Afghans were upset that an American soldier burned pages of the Koran. To do such a thing is seen as total disrespect to Allah and their country. Our movements are restricted to mission-essential travel only. I have learned to pray with a Jewish prayer shawl (called a Tallit) over my head as a symbol of humility before the Lord. Tonight as I was praying under my Tallit, the Spirit was interceding repeatedly with, "speak to my heart." These words were flowing in my heart during my worship.

As I realize the dangers of being in a combat zone, I don't want to become complacent and I cannot afford to be fearful. I know God is with me and He sends me encouraging words and experiences every day. As God continues **to speak to my heart**, I want to have my ears and heart open to learn of His divine comfort and care.

"For I the LORD thy God will hold thy right hand, saying unto thee, Fear not; I will help thee" (Isaiah 41:13).

23 February ~ "Awesome Artwork"

Today I was on a Compound tour with the Lead Operational Support Team Officer. While we were on the second level balcony, I noticed the beautiful mountains draped in white snow. I said to myself, "**Awesome artwork**, God. You are the ultimate artist. You are to be worshipped and praised for Your wonderful works and creations. There is none like You—I'm in awe of Your marvelous creations in nature!"

"I will remember the works of the LORD: surely I will remember thy wonders of old. I will meditate also of all thy work, and talk of thy doings. Thy way, O God, is in the sanctuary: who is so great a God as our God? Thou art the God that doest wonders: thou hast declared thy strength among the people. Thou hast with thine arm redeemed thy people, the sons of Jacob and Joseph. Selah" (Psalms 77:11-15).

24 February ~ "Where's Your Go Bag?"

We had live fire today! In other words, the enemy was shooting and we were in their path. I ran to get my rifle and IBA (individual body armor) and was on my way to a bunker when one of the Culture Advisors said, "The XO has to go to the Roof!" I didn't have my helmet or **go bag** with me. I realized I was unprepared and so I began to pray for protection. I had my radio and reported my location and who was with me. We were on lockdown for about 30 minutes before we got the "all clear."

When going to battle, a **go bag** should be prepared with everything you need on the battlefield—extra ammo, medical kit, blood chit, cleanup kit, etc. In the same way, Christians should pack their spiritual weapons for an impending spiritual battle (Ephesians 6:14).

In this version of the song, "Keep on the Firing Line,"[1] these words became alive:

If you're in the battle for the Lord and right,
Keep on the firing line;
If you win, my brother, surely you must fight,
Keep on the firing line;
There are many dangers that we all must face,
If we die still fighting it is no disgrace;
Cowards in the service will not find a place,
So keep on the firing line.

When we sang this song at my home church, Elder Lightfoot Solomon Michaux (the Founder of the Gospel Spreading Church of God) would ask the choir during a break in the song, "Are you ready for the battle, pilgrims?" This is the question we all need to

---

[1] Bessie F. Hatcher. *Keep on the Firing Line.* © Public Domain.

ask ourselves. Let's pack the right stuff! And don't leave home without **our go bags!**

"Finally, my brethren, be strong in the Lord, and in the power of his might. Put on the whole armour of God, that ye may be able to stand against the wiles of the devil. For we wrestle not against flesh and blood, but against principalities, against powers, against the rulers of the darkness of this world, against spiritual wickedness in high places. Wherefore take unto you the whole armour of God, that ye may be able to withstand in the evil day, and having done all, to stand. Stand therefore, having your loins girt about with truth, and having on the breastplate of righteousness; And your feet shod with the preparation of the gospel of peace; Above all, taking the shield of faith, wherewith ye shall be able to quench all the fiery darts of the wicked. And take the helmet of salvation, and the sword of the Spirit, which is the word of God: Praying always with all prayer and supplication in the Spirit, and watching thereunto with all perseverance and supplication for all saints" (Ephesians 6:10-18).

25 February ~ "Passionate About the Wrong Thing"

Most Afghan people are so passionate about the Koran. In spite of the fact that some cannot read it, the volume is still very sacred to them. The burning of the Koran this week caused uproar throughout Afghanistan. Their passion is admirable, but it is quite misplaced.

My prayer is that God will have compassion and deliver us all from the violence and disrespect of each other and what others believe. God is the one and only God. Even so, we must be careful to know and understand that our passion should be like that of Christ, who died for our sins. Our driving force should only be based on the Word of God. If you want to be passionate about something, let it be for the winning of souls to Christ for eternal life!

Two American soldiers were killed by Afghan soldiers today. I pray for peace in a land where many know neither peace nor the Prince of Peace! God have mercy!

"I am the LORD, and there is none else, there is no God beside me: I girded thee, though thou hast not known me: That they may know from the rising of the sun, and from the west, that there is none beside me. I am the

LORD, and there is none else. I form the light, and create darkness: I make peace, and create evil: I the LORD do all these things. Drop down, ye heavens, from above, and let the skies pour down righteousness: let the earth open, and let them bring forth salvation, and let righteousness spring up together; I the LORD have created it" (Isaiah 45:5-8).

26 February ~ "The Underappreciated Abundance"

This morning while I was washing up, I used my small travel-sized container of soft soap. I noticed that there was only a little left in the bottle. To compensate, I didn't use as much as I usually do when it is full. I have a large tube of toothpaste and I often put too much paste on my toothbrush. I guess I will become more stringent on my toothpaste use once that diminishes as well.

We don't truly appreciate God when we are in the land of abundance! It's only when things or people we depend on become sparse that we realize they are almost gone. In America, most enjoy an **abundance** of food, shelter, electricity, running water, wealth, air conditioning, heating, sanitation, etc. without giving it a second thought.

It is important to take time to appreciate what God has given us and use it wisely so that when it is gone, we know that we were good stewards while we had it in our possession.

This is also true about people in our lives—God gives us wonderful family members, pastors and friends. To appreciate them and not abuse or take their presence for granted will allow us not to have regrets when the day comes when they will no longer be in our presence. "Lord, I'm no longer going to take people or things for granted!"

"And the Lord said unto Moses, How long will this people provoke me? and how long will it be ere they believe me, for all the signs which I have shewed among them? I will smite them with the pestilence, and disinherit them, and will make of thee a greater nation and mightier than they" (Numbers 14:11-12).

26 February ~ "Not Too Old to be Teachable"

God has a few expectations that are non-negotiable. I am learning that He expects me to have a spirit of humility and a heart that is open to learn. This deployment is really teaching me some new skills about the business, myself, and learning to work with different personalities. But His expectation is that I will be open and willing to grow and learn during this time—even at my age!

I have to admit, I'm a little frustrated with the limited technology—it is definitely not like my home office. But God is showing me how to do things differently to get around the technological shortcomings and get similar results. PowerPoint?—I want SharePoint (my collaboration management software from home)! But we don't have it here. My new prayer, "God teach this old dog some new tricks!"

"Lead me in thy truth, and teach me: for thou art the God of my salvation; on thee do I wait all the day" (Psalms 25:5).

27 February ~ "Complacency Can Lead to Disaster"

We must remain vigilant and not let our guard down. The Bible tells us that *"the devil is like a roaring lion—seeking whom he may devour."* When we get **complacent**, we become numb to the devices of Satan. Then he will attack, causing a **disaster**.

The Taliban Insurgents are lurking, seeking what harm they can do to us. As people of God, we know Satan is busy and we must be ever so careful and watchful. We need to watch our souls and guard our minds so that he doesn't trip us and cause us to fall. It's like when an insurgent throws a grenade our way when we aren't looking, there can be devastating results. But if we are watchful, we can actually make them think twice about trying to harm us.

"In the same way, Lord, help me to be on my guard—checking my tongue, mind, soul and body that Satan will not find room to attack. This will surely please You, Lord!"

"Wherefore, beloved, seeing that ye look for such things, be diligent that ye may be found of him in peace, without spot, and blameless" (2 Peter 3:14).

27 February ~ "Not All At Once"

Today they did a mail run for the first time in a week or so, but there was nothing in the mailbag for me! It felt like Santa Claus came and didn't bring me anything. I know there had to be mail from home; I had clothes sent to me. Oh well, maybe tomorrow.

Sometimes, God does not give us everything that we want or those things we believe that are "due" to us. Often His blessings come a little here and a little there, spread out so we can appreciate them more. "Thank You, Lord for holding back my mail so I can appreciate my clothes more when they arrive." I am learning to make do with what I have—a little here and a little there.

"For ye have need of patience, that, after ye have done the will of God, ye might receive the promise" (Hebrews 10:36).

28 February ~ "A Little Hello"

Use what you have to bring great glory to God. **A little hello** can bring big results to a hurting soul. Use what God gave you (your gifts, your personality, and your talents) in order to bless someone else. I was talking to one young lady that had Charge of Quarters (CQ) duty last night and she mentioned that she speaks to people even when the situation could be fearful (like walking alone at night and a stranger passes by). You never know—your **little hello** could uplift the spirit and give God glory by making the difference in someone's day!

"Be kindly affectioned one to another with brotherly love; in honour preferring one another;" (Romans 12:10).

29 February ~ "God, You Take My Breath Away"

During my Tallit prayer, I experienced an awe-inspiring moment. **"God, You take my breath away** when I'm in Your Holy Presence! I can hardly breathe, but yet I am at peace—not laboring for air! Yes, just at peace and in awe of Your Holiness!" While on my knees under the covering of my prayer shawl, His presence was so overpowering that I could hardly breathe. I can't really explain it—there was no fear or desperation...just peace, calm and gratitude for being in His Chamber.

A breathless encounter with God made me realize my own unworthiness and God's passionate love for me. Below is Paul's encounter…

"It is not expedient for me doubtless to glory. I will come to visions and revelations of the Lord. I knew a man in Christ above fourteen years ago, (whether in the body, I cannot tell; or whether out of the body, I cannot tell: God knoweth;) such an one caught up to the third heaven. And I knew such a man, (whether in the body, or out of the body, I cannot tell: God knoweth;) How that he was caught up into paradise, and heard unspeakable words, which it is not lawful for a man to utter. Of such an one will I glory: yet of myself I will not glory, but in mine infirmities" (2 Corinthians 12:1-5).

29 February ~ "The Backseat View"

While riding with my Senior Logistician and Communications Technician in the city, the Senior Logistician was very focused on his driving. There were people everywhere in the street and the streets and off roads were very muddy! He was driving very aggressively—he told me that it was imperative to get through traffic and to try to avoid being near a military convoy due to their high visibility and probability of attack. From the **backseat,** I couldn't see what could impact our travel as I could only see the sights from the side windows. My view from the back was nerve racking.

Thank God He has a vantage point on high and looks below to see everything that's going on. He knows our front, back and sides and even what we are thinking—because He's omniscient. We can't see what's up ahead because **we're in the backseat** and that can be frustrating. However, God has control of the wheel and we need to sit back and enjoy the ride!

"Thou knowest my downsitting and mine uprising, thou understandest my thought afar off" (Psalms 139:2).

MARCH 2012

1 March ~ "Follow Your Instincts"

We had a power outage in the guard shack and water pump room today. It was hard to see where the breakers were while I was trying to help the technician. I said to myself, "See, I told you to take your flashlight, but you thought you didn't need it!"

When the still, small voice of God (1 Kings 19:12) tells you to do something—DO IT! Knowing the voice of God and the leading of the Holy Spirit is so important to success in life. It is better to be obedient than to suffer harsh consequences. I should have had my flashlight with me to help identify the problem and shine light where the technician was trying to see in the water pump room and guard shack. Lesson learned—I'll **follow my instincts** and add it to all the other stuff on my hip!

"But be ye doers of the word, and not hearers only, deceiving your own selves" (James 1:22).

2 March ~ "Accountability"

We had our Emergency Action Plan (EAP) exercise today. It took us 25 minutes to account for everyone on the Compound. As the Executive Officer (XO), I was responsible for contacting each rally station on the radio to get an accurate count of the number of people at each station. I messed up the numbers (double counted some folks) and I refused to call an end to the exercise until I got all the numbers correct. An after-action review revealed some changes we needed to make in our processes and the EAP plan.

We all must be accountable to someone. If we don't show up for work, we're AWOL (Absent Without Official Leave). This will cause our supervisor to call the "emergency contact" phone numbers you provided so they can ensure you're okay and accounted for.

Likewise, we are accountable to God. We will be judged according to our work here on Earth and stand before the throne of Christ and receive our just rewards.

"For many nations and great kings shall serve themselves of them also: and I will recompense them according to their deeds, and according to the works of their own hands" (Jeremiah 25:14).

3 March ~ "Which Weapon Should I Use?"

The first war was in heaven—God vs. Evil—more specifically— Pride! We are in a daily warfare against evil. We have to put on all the armor God has given to us daily. If I need it, I want to have my armor ready for protection. The armor that we get from the Holy Spirit is needed all day, every day!

I carry a long arm and a side arm; both have a specific purpose, depending on the situation you find yourself in. Side arms (9mm Sig Sauer) are used for close-up threats and targets. Long arms (M-4 Rifle) are used to eliminate targets and threats from a distance. Satan attacks us from all points and distances. If someone close to you is in your face attacking you, how do you respond? Pick from the arsenal available in His Word. If the person plots long-range barriers or stumbling blocks from a distance, be watchful. Pull from your spiritual arsenal to defend against the attacks of the devil.

"For we wrestle not against flesh and blood, but against principalities, against powers, against the rulers of the darkness of this world, against spiritual wickedness in high places" (Ephesians 6:12).

4 March ~ "Need to Get Regulated"

I didn't want to get up this morning! In fact, I got up, said my prayers and then retreated back to my bed. I really need to regulate my sleeping pattern here. Even though I get three meals per day, I don't always eat the Afghan cooked meals—I cheat and eat the food that I shipped from home.

I do need to give my body time to adjust to this new environment. I am 6,901 miles away from Baltimore, a nine-and-a-half hour time difference and 5,877 feet above sea level. I'm not quite sure how long it will take to **get regulated**, but for now, I'm tired. I thank God we have a late start time on Sundays.

I was thinking of our walk with Christ. We must **get regulated** to that life. We can't waver back and forth, being righteous in some things at the same time as having unrighteousness in other parts of our lives. Though the scriptures speak of a righteous man falling seven times, he eventually got up and got it together because he relied on God for strength and guidance. He became **regulated**. I'll get **regulated** physically and expand upon my spiritual walk day by day.

"For a just man falls seven times, and rises again, But the wicked stumble in time of calamity" (Proverbs 24:16).

4 March ~ "Lord Help Me Not to be Like Her"

I found myself working with a lady who has a definite Type A personality. You know the type—the people who are very competitive and boastful, who are aroused to anger easily and who are so goal driven, they feel a sense of urgency all the time. She tried to dominate and control everything and everyone on the Compound. I recognized it early—I could see it in her spirit (She would say, "Woe is me—people don't want to respond and work with me.") People alienate her because they don't want to deal with her constant criticism and curt comments.

I asked God to give me compassion and the right words to say. I will continue to try to work with her and one day help her to see the impact of her actions.

When you see yourself in someone else, it's hard to accept the fact that you act just like they do! In the mirror is one huge target. How do you break negative cycles of behavior or thoughts?

- First, recognize your own spirit, style, character and personality.
- Second, accept what you see.
- Third, repent for what is wrong.
- Fourth, put corrective actions in place.
- Fifth, be patient and compassionate with those who have not recovered. We would want them to extend the same patience and compassion to us.

God wants us to look in the mirror and see ourselves, acknowledge what we see and ask Him to help us change our ways.

"Therefore now amend your ways and your doings, and obey the voice of the Lord your God" (Jeremiah 26:13a).

5 March ~ "The Timer"

Each night, as instructed by Dr. Almeta Stokes, I go under the covering of my Tallit (prayer shawl) for five minutes. Dr. Stokes is a professor at Howard University and a prayer warrior in my church organization. She has the gift of healing and prays consistently, often utilizing her prayer shawl.

Prior to my departure, Dr. Stokes presented me with my very own prayer shawl during a women's power-hour of prayer session. Her guidance to pray for only five minutes was to teach me discipline and focus when approaching God's throne. I use my phone's timer to ensure I only pray for five minutes. I try to shut up and let God speak, but I often become distracted. It is hard—I always have something I want to say.

The timer went off at the set time of five minutes. We all are affected by **the timer**; we all have an appointed time. **The timer** is clicking and when God says ENOUGH, time will be no more for us here on Earth. We have appointed times for certain jobs or responsibilities. When the set time arrives, **the timer** will sound off and that job has ended—just like retirement.

We need to make the best of the time God has given us. As the seconds pass by, we should make every one of them count. When we stand before God at Judgment, we want Him to say, "Well done, good and faithful servant. You used every second I gave you to My honor and glory. Come be with me in my Kingdom."

Now, I understand that we don't always say nor do the right thing every second of the day. We are imperfect creatures, striving for perfection to make every second count towards our rewards in heaven. But **the timer** is counting down. "Lord, make me aware of Your will so I can be available to You and use my time wisely."

"To every thing there is a season, and a time to every purpose under the heaven: A time to be born, and a time to die; a time to plant, and a time to pluck up that which is planted;" (Ecclesiastes 3:1-2).

6 March ~ "Pray for the People of Afghanistan"

I'm always amazed at what I see while out and about. Today I saw old people, young women with babies, kids walking in the middle of the road, all begging for money and food. I pray for deliverance for these people in this country. YES, there are plenty of folks suffering in the U.S., but God wants me here to witness the plight of the Afghan people. I pray that all plans to harm and destroy these people are confused and foiled.

My prayer: "Lord, I ask that the suffering will end for the people of Afghanistan. I pray that they get the opportunity through the people visiting to know God. I ask that You will show folks Your way to help them learn of You and accept You as their Lord and Savior. These are souls that need salvation. I know how Jesus felt—there are so many, Lord, that need spiritual food. Allow me to break the bread and the fish as You did, so it will multiply and feed them. Grant me wisdom and knowledge of how and when to do so. Let me not offend them, but show love and compassion."

"For the poor shall never cease out of the land: therefore I command thee, saying, Thou shalt open thine hand wide unto thy brother, to thy poor, and to thy needy, in thy land" (Deuteronomy 15:11).

7 March ~ "No Two Are Alike"

While at the shooting range today, I was sitting on the ground waiting for my turn to practice the assigned shooting scenario. I was looking at the rocks and noticed that I couldn't find **two that were just alike**. They were of different shapes, colors and sizes. I was so intrigued; sitting there playing around with the rocks, holding and examining many of them—trying to find at least two that were similar. I could find none!

We too are unique creations made by God with different DNA. None of us are cloned. There are no two humans that are just alike—even identical twins have differences. We come in different sizes, shapes, personalities, ethnic backgrounds, cultures, etc. It is important to be confident in our shape and size and operate within the gift God has given us so that the Body of Christ is edified and God is glorified! We're like the sand on the sea shores. The following scriptures come to mind:

"For thou hast possessed my reins: thou hast covered me in my mother's womb. I will praise thee; for I am fearfully and wonderfully made: marvellous are thy works; and that my soul knoweth right well. My substance was not hid from thee, when I was made in secret, and curiously wrought in the lowest parts of the earth. Thine eyes did see my substance, yet being unperfect; and in thy book all my members were written, which in continuance were fashioned, when as yet there was none of them" (Psalms 139:13-16).

8 March ~ "I Will Show You (the Way)"

While I was listening during my Tallit prayer time, I heard: "I will show you the way, but will you follow?" My answer was: "Show me the way Lord, where You lead me, I will follow. Lead me; guide me along the way."

It is very easy to get lost here in Afghanistan. The maps are not that reliable and to make the most of your trip, ask an Afghan cultural advisor who knows the city and can guide and direct you safely to your destination. If you purchase a map to help you get to where you're going and decide instead to use your own judgment with directions instead of following the map, you probably won't get to your destination. You could get really lost or waste a lot of time in eventually getting there.

How many times has God given us direction as to what to do and where to go, and we don't follow Him? Why ask if you're not going to heed the guidance? Sometimes I think we go our own way because we don't TRUST GOD!

We must not frustrate the grace of God by being disobedient. God loves us and wants to continually provide us with blessings. He would not lead us on a path of destruction—the wrong way. Even though we don't see familiar landmarks on this journey, TRUST God to be the Guide. Yes, He is willing to show us the way, but we have to have the mindset to be led and follow. It's not easy; we want it our way and we think we know what's best. Don't ask God for direction if you're not going to follow His guidance.

"And the LORD shall guide thee continually, and satisfy thy soul in drought, and make fat thy bones: and thou shalt be like a watered garden, and like a spring of water, whose waters fail not" (Isaiah 58:11).

8 March ~ "The No-Show Fairy"

My daughter Christina and my friend Allison posted Facebook entries about the **tooth fairy**. Two wonderful, loving and caring moms somehow botched the whole tooth fairy plan with their first graders, losing points with their sons. The **tooth fairy** is a fairy tale!! My grandson, Isaiah exclaimed: "You're a fake tooth fairy!" The money was not under his pillow as the fairy tale was told it would be.

Sometimes we live in a fantasy world where we think some little creature with wings will fly into our lives and give us what we want or desire. You're right Isaiah. The tooth fairy is not real. But God is no fairy tale! He will show up on time, when you need Him, where He's needed. *"God is a Spirit: and they that worship Him must worship Him in spirit and in truth."* (John 4:24)

Satan specializes in fairy tales, making fools out of people over and over again. He makes promises that he doesn't plan to keep. He will lead you out into the dark waters and drop you like a hot potato. Satan is real and no joke, but he doesn't have pixie dust on his wand.

We know that God is truth and every man a liar (Romans 3:4). He means what He says—He will show up! He's not bringing money for your lost tooth, but gives freely of His Spirit.

"God forbid: yea, let God be true, but every man a liar; as it is written, That thou mightest be justified in thy sayings, and mightest overcome when thou art judged" (Romans 3:4).

9 March ~ "Closer to Heaven Here"

It is customary to celebrate the arrival of new people to the Compound and say farewell to those who are leaving. This celebration is known as a Hail and Farewell. One night we had our hail and farewell celebration outside in the cold, around the fire pit. While I was wrapped in my jacket, I had the opportunity to look UP! Wow, what a show! The sky was so near; the stars were so vivid. Two planets were so bright. The Little Dipper and Big Dipper were clear as day. My thought was: "Afghanistan is **closer to Heaven** than anywhere that I've been. The heavens seem so reachable."

I thought about this country with its mountains. Afghanistan is part of the earth that God made—and He said it was good. There once was a time when this land was beautiful with vegetation and flowing water from the mountains. I believe Afghanistan was created to be a beautiful place for people to live. God's creation was perfect in design. It was through war and man's lust for control that destroyed so much of its beauty. Yet, the sky remains in its original beauty and reflects the God who made it.

"To whom then will ye liken me, or shall I be equal? saith the Holy One. Lift up your eyes on high, and behold who hath created these things, that bringeth out their host by number: he calleth them all by names by the greatness of his might, for that he is strong in power; not one faileth" (Isaiah 40:25-26).

10 March ~ "Prepare Tonight for Tomorrow Is Coming"

This teachable moment is dedicated to my niece Tara Smith who gave it to me.

Learning to prepare the night before for the next day takes time—it's a skill that is learned. It has to do with time management. Experience is a great teacher! Doing so will reap benefits in the morning! When you don't have to rush, if something goes wrong tomorrow, you'll have time to adjust and refocus on the morning tasks.

Jesus told us to prepare for His coming. We should always be ready for His coming. That means to *"be ye also ready."* We need to prepare through our works but our hearts must also be right, and our consciences should be clear. We need to be filled with His Spirit, and have our armor ready for a moment's notice.

I have my clothes at the foot of my bed. My helmet, my assault rifle, and my IBA (Individual Body Armor) are on a stand and easily accessible, ready for action if the situation presents itself.

No man knows the day or the hour, but we must be ready. The only way to be ready is to prepare every night, each day, every hour and minute. Ask God to keep you day by day—guard your heart, mind, soul and body for that great resurrection day.

"Let your loins be girded about, and your lights burning; And ye yourselves like unto men that wait for their lord, when he will return from the wedding; that when he cometh and knocketh, they may open unto him immediately. Blessed are those servants, whom the lord when he cometh shall find watching: verily I say unto you, that he shall gird himself, and make them to sit down to meat, and will come forth and serve them. And if he shall come in the second watch, or come in the third watch, and find them so, blessed are those servants. And this know, that if the goodman of the house had known what hour the thief would come, he would have watched, and not have suffered his house to be broken through. Be ye therefore ready also: for the Son of man cometh at an hour when ye think not" (Luke 12:35- 40).

10 March ~ "Get Rid of the Germs"

Lots of people are sick with runny noses, coughing, etc. Everyone who works in Charge of Quarters (CQ) at night gets some kind of germ. We need a good cleaning! I asked the First Sergeant to get the house staff to wipe down door knobs and common areas daily with disinfectant. We need to get rid of this germ floating in the air that is infecting these people.

An evil spirit is like a germ, floating around, transferring from one body to the next, and infecting everyone it touches. The blood of Jesus can cleanse us and wash away the evil spirits, just as we can wash our hands and faces to purify our bodies and remove the germs. Jesus' blood has the same effect but is much more powerful. We were washed and made whole inside as well as out. Don't let the evil spirit infiltrate your mind and body. It will make you sick and spiritual sickness is deadly.

We use hand sanitizer to rid our bodies of germs. Likewise, we are to cleanse our hands and bodies of the filthiness of the flesh with spiritual "sanitizer." Instead of depending on a product that will remove 99% of the germs, we can accept the lasting Savior who can remove 100% of the filth through His blood and the renewing of our mind. "Live germ free!"

"Having therefore these promises, dearly beloved, let us cleanse ourselves from all filthiness of the flesh and spirit, perfecting holiness in the fear of God" (2 Corinthians 7:1).

11 March ~ "The Importance of Friends"

This is dedicated to my best friend forever (BFF), Donna Gray.
I sent a text to Donna this morning after re-reading a card she sent me. I was thinking of her and our friendship. The Bible says, *"A man that hath friends must shew himself friendly: and there is a friend that sticketh closer than a brother"* (Proverbs 18:24).

Donna is that kind of friend! We have been through thick and thin together; each of us went through the times of dating, marriage, raising our children, sending them off to college and helping my girls with their wedding plans. We've laughed, cried, and had much fun together.

Never underestimate the **importance** of having good, strong, faithful **friends**. Abraham was a **friend** of God (2 Chronicles 20:7). A **friend** loves at all times (Proverbs 17:17). It is also important to rightly treat your friends—reciprocate that respect, love and care.

We should make known to each other things (share knowledge and wisdom) that God has given us. Friends are important—"I love You BFF!!" Jesus said:

"Henceforth I call you not servants; for the servant knoweth not what his lord doeth; but I have called you friends; for all things that I have heard of my Father I have made known unto you" (John 15:15).

11 March ~ "Distance Makes the Heart Grow Fonder"

This is definitely a true saying. I miss my hubby! There's nothing wrong with our marriage, but I believe this deployment will teach each of us the love and appreciation we have for each other. Thirty-three years is a long time to be together. Only by God's grace and mercy—teaching me to compromise, take the low road, be submissive (yes, I said it), break the ice first, and learn to love and respect Frank for who he is.

Being so far away for such a long time has been difficult, but I'm determined to make it back home to see Frank, the children and everyone soon. Just as my relationship with Christ must grow stronger and deeper, so shall our marriage. When we are apart, we long for each other. I know this has not been easy for him. I enjoy the wacky texts we send to each other, erupting fresh thoughts and playful care for one another. I miss you Frank and can't wait to get back home to you.

"Let him kiss me with the kisses of his mouth: for thy love is better than wine" (Song of Solomon 1:2).

11 March ~ "Hey, My Satellite Signal Has Zapped"

When it rains or snows, our satellite connection is either spotty or non-existent. No TV signal—that's hard for anyone to handle in this day and age! In the same way, when we allow anything to come between us and God, our connection with Him can become spotty or not exist at all. Restore my connection, Lord! Our connection with God must be free of interference. We must take gossip, complaining, disobedience, discontentment, distractions, etc. out of our lives. "God, can you hear me now? I want to hear You clearly!"

"Restore unto me the joy of Your Salvation, and uphold me with thy free spirit" (Psalms 51:12).

12 March ~ "The Mountains that Touch the Sky!"

My flight to Kandahar today was canceled after I got to the airport—oh well. But, I did have the opportunity to take pictures of the gorgeous mountains. There were mountains on top of mountains and behind the mountains were even more snow-capped mountains. The mountains that reached the sky and clouds caught my attention. Of course, I've never seen such stunning views of God's handiwork—so I was in awe and amazed. Even the mountains reach up to give God Glory!

As I studied the mountain peaks, valleys and crevices, I could only imagine these mountains as hill tops at one time long ago. I also imagined God standing on them melting and splitting them (Micah 1:4). This was a vivid visualization of this scripture. The makeup of these mountains had deep cuts, where the waters from melted snow ran down to the valley. Micah was referring to God's judgment on Samaria regarding worshipping carnal images (idols). He said that *"God will tread on the high places of the earth."*

The mountains can unfold to reveal so many revelations; you just have to study and be quiet and let God talk to you.

"The mountains melt like wax at the presence of the Lord" (Psalms 97:5).

13 March ~ "In the Multitude of Counselors, There's Safety"

I had to call a late 2030 hours meeting with the right subject matter experts (SMEs) at the table to discuss some issues. The meeting went well with the SMEs giving their guidance and telling me that I need to make the decision regarding the issues we discussed.

You must get the right people at the table for a discussion, and then you'll get the expert advice needed to make a decision. Proverbs 11:14 (see below) is a verse I often quote at work because I believe in it wholeheartedly!

Decisions that I make must have the safety and security of our Compound occupants in mind. I can't just make decisions and changes without considering everyone and I can't make them solely on my own without the benefit of others' input. This is true in spiritual life as well. We can't just make it into heaven on our own—we must have the Holy Spirit, who is our guide, counselor and friend. When we must make a decision, we must do it with God's counsel.

Get His input when you're in trouble, need to make a large purchase, or have family or mental issues. Let God direct you to the source of counseling needed for your situation. Plans and purposes will fail or be disappointing without SME counseling. God said to *"ask and it shall be given to you."* He also says that *"if anyone lacks wisdom, He will give it freely—but we must ask in faith"* (James 1:5). Don't go it alone.

"Where no counsel is, the people fall: but in the multitude of counsellors there is safety" (Proverbs 11:14).

"Without counsel purposes are disappointed: but in the multitude of counsellors they are established" (Proverbs 15:22).

"For by wise counsel thou shalt make thy war: and in multitude of counsellors [there is] safety" (Proverbs 24:6).

14 March ~ "Safe Travels Over the Dangerous Highways"

I traveled to Mazar-e Sharif today on a C-130 military aircraft. I also received a deeper meaning of **dangerous highways**. The reality of traveling on dangerous highways is that there are people who sit and wait to do you harm. "God, confuse and diffuse the plans of the enemy to do harm and evil."

Not only are the highways here busy and chaotic, but they also have no traffic signals nor marked lanes on most major roads. We were taught to pray prior to traveling and thank God upon return. These prayers, and those of my family, have kept me safe thus far over these perilous highways.

"The LORD shall preserve thee from all evil: he shall preserve thy soul. The LORD shall preserve thy going out and thy coming in from this time forth, and even for evermore" (Psalms 121:7-8).

14 March ~ "Oh No, My Windshield Wiper Fluid is Empty"

Afghan roads are mostly horrible and muddy, with potholes the size of a tire. The drivers are never concerned about getting the vehicles dirty—they constantly wash the windshields because of the volume of dirty water, mud, etc. that is always on them. A majority of the vehicles on the road are covered with mud. Front, sides, and backs—even windows are covered. Some Afghan drivers hang their heads out the window to see, because they have no fluid to clean their windshields.

The story of the 10 virgins (five wise and five foolish) fits this teachable moment. It's part of our Vehicle Movement Standard Operating Procedures for the vehicles to have sufficient supply of elements required to be safe.

If we have drivers who leave the Compound without checking the vehicle prior to departure, they are held responsible if they get in a situation where they may need something like windshield wiper fluid and the vehicle's tank is empty. Don't leave home without it! At the time and moment you think you're okay, you'll need the wiper fluid and it won't be there—causing you to miss your turn, hit something or somebody because you can't see.

This situation refers to the five foolish virgins who took no extra oil and needed it when the bridegroom came. The five wise had extra and was able to get in when the bridegroom came. Be wise, fill up and check prior to your departure. Keep the Holy Spirit thriving in your life so He can guide and teach you when you need it.

"And five of them were wise, and five were foolish. They that were foolish took their lamps, and took no oil with them: But the wise took oil in their vessels with their lamps" (Matthew 25:2-4).

15 March ~ "Why Carry the Weight?"

As a requirement to fly on military aircraft, you must wear your individual body armor (IBA) and a helmet. The IBA vest has plates weighing about 35 pounds. The vest without the plates weighs approximately two pounds. I sat at the airport for three and half hours because my flight was delayed. I had my IBA on the entire time! It's cumbersome, heavy and difficult to put on and take off without help. So I normally leave it on. Then of course I'm uncomfortable, and can't get in a good sitting position. I thought to myself: "Why are you carrying this weight unnecessarily?"

Some people **carry the weight** of sin, guilt, and anger for no apparent reason. If this is you, why not rip off the vest of sin and be free to move about with ease? Once the weight is off, you'll feel so much better…lighter. Let God remove the weight by choosing life and freedom. Saying "NO" to the devil and sin takes determination! You must accept Jesus as your Savior and not return to that sin. It's a choice that everyone must make. Why not be free today?

"Wherefore seeing we also are compassed about with so great a cloud of witnesses, let us lay aside every weight, and the sin which doth so easily beset us, and let us run with patience the race that is set before us," (Hebrews 12:1).

16 March ~ "Walgreens, I Miss You"

The days of running to the corner Walgreens are gone for five more months. Those things that we depend on due to the convenience of being right there can just disappear. I don't have the luxury of going to the local CVS, Walgreens or other pharmacy to get medications.

I have to put on my Individual Body Armor (IBA), carry my sidearm, and ask a driver and gunner to go out onto dangerous roads to get to a Post Exchange (PX) with limited supplies. After all it took to get there—risking life and limb (mine and two others); there were NO tissues on the shelves! I almost threw a temper tantrum because I wanted the luxury of Walgreens to get relief from my nasal condition!

This mission is so real! God has fortified me and helped me adapt to bare minimum conditions—I'm getting there, kicking and screaming. I quickly got over it and settled on the toilet tissue. Thank God for at least having toilet tissue!

Sometimes we take for granted the finer things in life, including God's blessings. I can share my experiences in these pages, but unless you have walked in my shoes, you might not be motivated or enthused about this teachable moment. The main point I want you to take away from this thought is: "Appreciate God's blessings of convenience and simplicity while you can enjoy them—they could one day disappear."

"Bless the LORD, O my soul: and all that is within me, bless his holy name. Bless the LORD, O my soul, and forget not all his benefits: Who forgiveth all thine iniquities; who healeth all thy diseases; Who redeemeth thy life from destruction; who crowneth thee with lovingkindness and tender mercies; Who satisfieth thy mouth with good things; so that thy youth is renewed like the eagle's" (Psalms 103:1-5).

17 March ~ "The Hands that Cut Your Hair"

Today I got my first haircut by a Filipino male barber. Well, there's a first time for everything! He was very gentle, patient and precise in cutting away what I didn't need and shape up what was left. While sitting in the chair, I was totally at the mercy of his hands.

We are in God's hands! He will sit us in the chair of life and purge us from the immorality we shouldn't have in our lives. Then He can cut away, shape and mold us into His image. The finished product is fearfully and wonderfully made. A beautiful image made just for the Master's use. Whew—I feel like a new woman!

"So God created man in his own image, in the image of God created he him; male and female created he them" (Genesis 1:27).

18 March ~ "The Devil's No-Harm Program/False Sense of Security"

While on Charge of Quarters (CQ) duty, I was watching the cameras which also monitored areas outside the gate. I remember the Operational Support Team Lead telling me during orientation to never go outside the gate on foot for anything. From merely watching the cameras, I might think things seem safe and okay; no one looks suspicious. But if I go outside the gate, I don't really know who could be watching and waiting for some curious soul to step out onto their territory. I could be kidnapped or shot!

Satan has a program that has been successful for a long time: "It's okay, no one is watching. Go outside the gate and explore the outside world." BAM!! The next thing you know, you're a statistic! The world has many devices to offer and tempt you—they're traps for a nonchalant Christian ignorant of Satan's devices. BE SMART! Listen to the guidance of your parents and other leaders who have your best interest at heart. I know the devil's offers are temping, but they are dangerous. Don't be fooled into believing that there's no harm in Satan's **"No-Harm program."**

He's *"roaming to and fro, seeking whom he may devour."* Stay behind the security gate!

"For the Lord giveth wisdom: out of his mouth cometh knowledge and understanding. He layeth up sound wisdom for the righteous: he is a buckler to them that walk uprightly. He keepeth the paths of judgment, and preserveth the way of his saints" (Proverbs 2:6-8).

19 March ~ "Tempted by Curiosity"

Today is my 53rd birthday! I was elated to receive cards from my best friend Donna Gray, and my brother Peter and his wife Ernestine Smith. How interesting it was that there would be Afghan fireworks (in honor of my birthday?) tonight! When I heard fireworks and, I have to admit, I was **tempted** to go watch. After all, **curiosity** is human nature. I was **curious** to see how the Afghans display their fireworks, and therefore tempted to go see them from the rooftop; this was yet another trick of the enemy.

Sometimes **curiosity** will get us to the edge and the temptation that may follow will take us out on the precarious ledge. Learn to listen to the small, still voice of God that says, "Not a good idea, stay put, you don't need to see the event!" *"Obedience is better than sacrifice"* (1 Samuel 15:22). Satan will always take you to the edge, just as he did with Jesus during His 40-day fast. Satan tried to tempt Jesus by showing Him all that he said could be His (Luke 4:1-13).

Satan will tempt you when you are weak. To be curious is one thing, but to fall into temptation is another thing. Don't allow Satan to get you by itching your **curiosity** to do something or go somewhere that you know deep down inside is wrong. Pleasure given to the flesh for even a moment could lead down a road toward eternal damnation.

"When wisdom entereth into thine heart, and knowledge is pleasant unto thy soul; Discretion shall preserve thee, understanding shall keep thee: To deliver thee from the way of the evil man, from the man that speaketh froward things;" (Proverbs 2:10-12).

20 March ~ "Our Actions Drive Perceptions"

When we allow Satan to get us riled up and angry, we get on the defensive and strike back. Often, what is in our hearts goes straight to the rooftop for all to see. *"Be angry and sin not"* (Ephesians 4:26). We "explode" because we do not allow the Holy Spirit to bring peace to that situation. Once you deny Him access, you're out there looking and sounding stupid. People see and hear your reactions to a situation and immediately draw a perception of who they think you are. Temperance is a learned skill, so be cool!

I know I'll have to eat these words—"Lord, help me when my turn comes. For Your glory and honor, let me shine a positive light on the life I claim to live."

"Suffer not thy mouth to cause thy flesh to sin; neither say thou before the angel, that it was an error: wherefore should God be angry at thy voice, and destroy the work of thine hands?" (Ecclesiastes 5:6).

21 March ~ "Trust in God"

Since I worked Charge of Quarters (CQ) last night, I had the opportunity to sleep in a little. I was thinking and preparing myself for travel and flight to Kandahar, where we just recently experienced violence. There was an uprising by the Afghans due to bad actions on the part of a military service member. I remember Frank telling to me to stay out of Kandahar due to what he saw on TV. I had to make a decision whether to stay on the Compound or continue with my travel plans.

Nothing is impossible when you put your **trust in God**. Trusting Him is putting a situation in His hands and leaving it there. Trusting Him is like a child who jumps into the pool into his parent's arms. Trusting Him is like Peter, focusing on Jesus while taking the walk of faith on the water to Him. Trusting Him is like falling backwards into the arms of a strong loved one.

He won't leave you nor forsake you. He won't drop you or lead you astray—just put your **trust in God**!

"Trust in the LORD with all thine heart; and lean not unto thine own understanding. In all thy ways acknowledge him, and he shall direct thy paths" (Proverbs 3:5-6).

22 March ~ "You Prayed…God Answered"

Today I traveled to Kandahar on the Dash 45—a super-light sized business jet aircraft produced by Bombardier Aerospace. Brand-new, the Dash 45 costs around U.S. $11.5 million. The flight was calm and the view of the snow-capped mountains was breath taking! Once on the ground, I received a detailed brief prior to going on to the next site visit. The brief was similar to my Individual Protective Measures Training, which covers what to do if the occupants of the vehicle became separated due to an incident. The British officer drove aggressively and fast!

The gunner, who was on the right-hand passenger side, called into the office periodically at certain checkpoints to report on our status. We were almost there when there was a loud explosion! Fire, smoke, and debris soared about 100 feet

in the air; the vehicle rocked from side to side. We could feel the heat of the fire and explosion. The British driver yelled: "Florence, pick up your weapon!" and then, "Look for secondaries!" There was smoke and dust so thick that we couldn't see the road. The British driver did an outstanding job controlling the vehicle and getting us out of harm's way quickly. There was a big oil rig which we thought would be the secondary explosion—the driver was able to get around it and almost slammed into the back of a donkey-drawn wagon carrying women and children. He maneuvered the vehicle skillfully to get around them as well.

Though it happened quickly, it seemed like slow motion. When I saw an iron gate or door flying about 100 feet in the air, I prayed, "Lord, please don't let that gate fall on us!" He answered! Due to the loudness and pressure of the explosion, my right ear felt muffled and I heard only a buzz. We all asked each other if we were okay. We were calm, yet startled—shocked!

"The angel of the LORD encampeth round about them that fear him, and delivereth them" (Psalms 34:7).

"Thank You, Lord, for your divine protection from dangers seen and unseen!" That request was realized at a level as never before in my life. I said I wanted to do something adventurous in my life while I still had the energy, health and strength, but...not in this manner.

When we arrived at our destined location, I called Charge of Quarters (CQ) to check in and told the security team what happened. Later, I received a Tandberg (video conference) call from my boss in the States. He'd already heard about the incident, since all incidents of this type must be documented and notifications must be made to the leadership. He wanted to ensure I was handling the situation calmly and that I was not hurt. I told him my life was in God's hands and I was okay. He said all the right things...call if you need counseling, etc. He said I would have resulting emotional stress later. I thought, "Yeah right...I know who my Redeemer is and my life is in His hands." I thanked him for the call and his concern. The only effect I experienced was a headache and muffled feeling in my right ear. I took a pain killer and felt better.

When the group of guys at the site sat around the conference room table and discussed the incident, I told them that things happen for a reason and that God protected us from harm. I mentioned how I always pray when I get in a vehicle asking God for protection and safe travels; then thank Him when I arrive.

The lesson I learned today was to be careful for what I ask, because I just might get it... plus some! What an adventure! I thought about how my entire family on the East Coast and Midwest was praying for my safety. Even though I could not tell my family and friends of this incident at the time, **God answered their prayers!** I actually felt the impact of the prayers of the righteous.

"But now thus saith the LORD that created thee, O Jacob, and he that formed thee, O Israel, Fear not: for I have redeemed thee, I have called thee by thy name; thou art mine. When thou passest through the waters, I will be with thee; and through the rivers, they shall not overflow thee: when thou walkest through the fire, thou shalt not be burned; neither shall the flame kindle upon thee" (Isaiah 43:1-2).

"The effectual fervent prayer of a righteous man availeth much" (James 5:16b).

22 March ~ "Look for Secondaries"

During the Vehicle Borne Improvised Explosive Device (VBIED) bombing today, we were told to **look for secondaries**—other opportunities for the enemy to bomb us in case the first one didn't kill us!

Satan is not a "one shot and forget" enemy. He will attack us with something big to throw us off guard and then double back with another hit when we are stunned and not paying attention. Be on the lookout for secondary attempts to trip you. Ask God to assist you in absorbing the initial blow to stay on guard. Sometimes big blows in life can rock you so hard that you can lose focus and find it hard to regain your composure.

In our weakness, He will make us strong. You have to be in tune to the Spirit to allow a rebound. Pick yourself up, brush yourself off, and get back in the battle.

"Lest Satan should get an advantage of us: for we are not ignorant of his devices" (2 Corinthians 2:11).

22 March ~ "Be Careful What You Ask For"

We can sometimes ask for things without considering the full or resulting consequences. I'm not sure of my motivation in saying, "I wanted to do something adventurous," other than doing something different, out of my norm and outside the box. Know and confront your motives when you ask God for something. You could get more than you asked for.

The adventure of being deep in the land and roadways of the Taliban was not exactly what I meant when I was looking for an adventure. But God took me through the dangerous areas; even though it was a potentially fatal explosion, we were unharmed. The explosion we experienced was definitely an adventure that I survived, but didn't really desire.

By no means was my quest for adventure comparable to the Israelites. During their adventure, they began complaining about food while they wandered in the wilderness. (Read Exodus 16:4-8.) The lesson learned is to not forget the works of God in my life and **be careful** of the desires of my heart.

"They soon forgat his works; they waited not for his counsel: But lusted exceedingly in the wilderness, and tempted God in the desert. And he gave them their request; but sent leanness into their soul" (Psalms 106:13-15).

23 March ~ "Put Your Helmet On"

While on the helicopter today, I noticed that I was the only one (besides the guy next to me) without my helmet on. It's regulation to wear it during flight. I was ignorant and just didn't realize I didn't have the helmet on. Once I did (duh), I got in compliance!

I thought about our journey/flight to heaven; everyone with their crowns on and I'm there, the only one with it in my hands. Pay attention! Don't be distracted—the crown has a purpose. I shall wear a crown!

"Henceforth there is laid up for me a crown of righteousness, which the Lord, the righteous judge, shall give me at that day: and not to me only, but unto all them also that love his appearing" (2 Timothy 4:8).

23 March ~ "Guard Your Gun"

We were trained to never put the gun down and leave it unattended. It is our protector from the enemy and harm. If left unattended, someone could pick it up and report it as a lost weapon; or the enemy could take it and use it against you. Both situations are not good.

The Holy Spirit is our weapon of protection against the enemy. We must guard our relationship with the Holy Spirit as if our life depends on it, because it does. We cannot survive without it. We can't face or defeat the enemy without it. It's like a soldier on the battlefield confronting the enemy without a weapon.

Beware of your surroundings and guard your heart. Don't let anyone or anything get between you and your Protector.

"So shall they fear the name of the LORD from the west, and his glory from the rising of the sun. When the enemy shall come in like a flood, the Spirit of the LORD shall lift up a standard against him" (Isaiah 59:19).

23 March ~ "When You Call and Don't Get an Answer"

I missed my travel partner at the time we were to meet to go back to the office. I called him and **got no answer**. I called my colleague *five times* and got no answer! So there I was, standing out on the sidewalk, not knowing how to contact anyone. "Somebody HELP ME!" I cried within...

We get that way sometimes with God. It seems like we can't get through and we're out in the wilderness all alone and can't reach our mother, father, or friend. SOMEBODY HELP ME! I am thankful for the Word of God, in which I can always find comfort.

When you're at the point that you have to depend solely on God, fret not. He's there—just hang in there! He will ANSWER.

"Let your conversation be without covetousness; and be content with such things as ye have: for he hath said, I will never leave thee, nor forsake thee. So that we may boldly say, The Lord is my helper, and I will not fear what man shall do unto me" (Hebrews 13: 5-6).

23 March ~ "The TGI Fridays Perpetrator"

You can't judge a book by its cover. It looked like **TGI Fridays;** it was decorated like Fridays, and had the same name on the door. But, they didn't have everything like the **TGI Fridays** at home. I heard so much about the Boardwalk at Kandahar and all its restaurants. I thought, a **Fridays**—GREAT, I want a pecan crusted chicken salad. Much to my dismay, they didn't have the salad and the meal that I did order tasted awful. It was not of the quality I was accustomed to at Friday's at home. I was very disappointed!

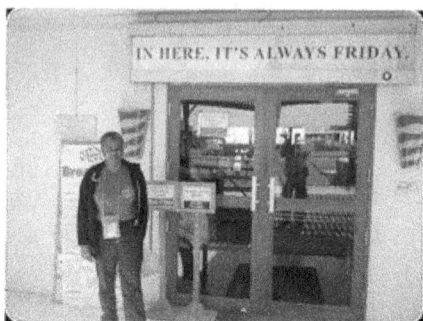

Satan is very skilled at making people seem like they are Christians when they are actually enemy perpetrators! They are wolves in sheep's clothing. If it looks like a duck and quacks like a duck—it must be a duck, right? Not always... Be careful!

I heard this saying when I was a child: "Be what you are and live the life. God knows your heart and you can't get by. He's coming back to judge the world. Be what you are and live the life." Be real, genuine—God's light will show through you before the world. Be authentic!

"Be sober, be vigilant; because your adversary the devil, as a roaring lion, walketh about, seeking whom he may devour." (1 Peter 5:8).

23 March ~ "Routine Maintenance"

Today I took my first helicopter ride ... it was cool! It was a Boeing CH-47 Chinook, a 14-seater with two pilots, two helpers and 10 passengers. We made two stops—for drop-offs and refueling. It was a wonderful experience and safe ride, unlike my trip the day before. Despite the fact that choppers are sometimes grounded due to Taliban snipers trying to pluck them out of the sky and disrupt operations, I arrived safely to my destination.

As I stood on the side of the airfield waiting for the maintenance crew to refuel the chopper, I thought about how we need to refuel spiritually. We must conduct **routine maintenance** of our spiritual mind, body and soul to ensure we are "fit" for the spiritual battle we face daily. Our **routine maintenance** involves daily prayer, seeking God through reading His Word, worship and fasting. These actions will grease our armor and make us ready for whatever Satan throws at us. Staying fit is essential to winning the battle. Let's keep our **routine maintenance** an integral part of our daily rituals.

"Glory ye in his holy name: let the heart of them rejoice that seek the LORD. Seek the LORD and his strength, seek his face continually" (1 Chronicles 16:10-11).

24 March ~ "Space A"

"Space A" is short for "space available." This means if space is available, you can get on the flight. I was exhausted and just wanted to get out of Kandahar and get back to Kabul.

I prayed and asked God to let us get a **"Space A"** seat on the flight back to Kabul. He did just that! I continued in prayer as such: "Thank You God for answering my simple prayer. Thank You for bringing us over the airways safely to the Compound." Even though I can't, for security reasons, inform my family right now about being attacked by insurgents with a Vehicle Borne Improvised Explosive Device, I feel the prayers of my church and family members. God, I thank You for Your loving arms surrounding me, keeping me day by day."

I thank God for my **"Space A"** seat in the congregation of the righteous! I'm so grateful that there's room at the cross for me.

"(To the chief Musician, Altaschith, Michtam of David, when he fled from Saul in the cave.) Be merciful unto me, O God, be merciful unto me: for my soul trusteth in thee: yea, in the shadow of thy wings will I make my refuge, until these calamities be overpast" (Psalms 57:1).

24 March ~ "Yuck, My Bag is Dirty"

One thing I hate is when I get my stuff dirty. I don't want to touch it or be near it! During my travels, I got **my bag dirty**. It is dusty everywhere you go in Afghanistan, so it is almost impossible to keep anything that you wear or carry clean.

God hates the dirt of sin…He will NOT allow it in His Kingdom!

"Come now, and let us reason together, saith the LORD: though your sins be as scarlet, they shall be as white as snow; though they be red like crimson, they shall be as wool" (Isaiah 1:18).

24 March ~"The View from the Rear"

We're always looking and reaching forward in our general and spiritual lives. But, it is good to have a **view from the rear**.

The concept of a rear view became clear to me as we were escorted like cattle into the rear of the C-130 aircraft to take our seats. While waiting to take off, I was looking out the rear of this aircraft. Everyone and everything is loaded from the rear. The pilot area must stay clear of movement to focus on where we are going.

We, too, must keep our front sight clear so we can see where we are going. When we look back and see where God has brought us from, it's such a humbling sight. From **a rear view**, we can assess how things happened and then play "Monday Morning Quarterback," or how things could have been done differently from the vantage of hindsight. These are lessons learned; experiences from which we can grow and develop.

The **view from the rear** can be fatal, especially if, when you look back, you desire to go back to a sinful life. Remember Lot's wife. She looked back due to her love of her friends and home. She wanted to see what happened to the city. Not only did she look back in her heart, she physically looked back. We must guard our hearts so that we don't look back to go back. The **view from the rear** has its place.

"And it came to pass, when they had brought them forth abroad, that he said, Escape for thy life; look not behind thee, neither stay thou in all the plain; escape to the mountain, lest thou be consumed. But his wife looked back from behind him, and she became a pillar of salt" (Genesis 19:17, 26).

25 March ~ "Uncomfortable Ride"

I traveled to Herat today. The flight was delayed two hours, but thank God we arrived safely on the C-130 aircraft.

It was sad to see the soldiers with all their gear on trying to get in a good, comfortable position to sleep during the flight while sitting in the jump seats. I didn't try to sleep. I was too busy looking around to be cognizant of my surroundings, observing the others and making notes as I traveled. I, too, was uncomfortable with all my gear. I placed my M-4 rifle on the floor to keep it from slipping from my grasp and held it with my feet. It was cold! The plane was loud and sometimes quite bumpy.

We sometimes long for our heavenly home where comfort is a reality and everlasting. Don't get comfortable here—we're not here to stay. This is not our true home—it is only temporal. Don't become complacent and settle on Earth, for God has prepared a place for us to forever be with Him.

"For our light affliction, which is but for a moment, worketh for us a far more exceeding and eternal weight of glory; While we look not at the things which are seen, but at the things which are not seen: for the things which are seen are temporal; but the things which are not seen are eternal" (2 Corinthians 4:17-18).

26 March ~ "Refuel the Fire"

Since our flight was canceled, I had the opportunity to see the city and downtown Herat. It was clean and had trees (unlike Kabul) and I even saw a camel parked in front of a building built by Alexander the Great.

In the evening, we had dinner near the fire pit. While standing by the fire pit watching the fire burn, one gentleman began poking it to stir up the contents and **refuel** the flames. I began to think while I watched.

If you don't add fuel or contents to a fire that is already aflame, it will soon die or go out. Poking it and reshuffling the contents that fueled it will keep it going a little longer, but eventually you'll need additional wood, coal or whatever is used to burn the fire.

Our spirit needs to be refueled constantly to keep the Holy Spirit burning in our hearts. As the Holy Spirit is resident dwelling in us, every now and then we need a poke to keep the fire burning. Worship, being spiritually fed through a workshop or seminar, a prayer breakfast, prayer sessions, encounters, or ministry work all help poke us. If we do not fuel our spiritual container, the fire will eventually be extinguished and go out. We will no longer be able to provide light or heat. Our spiritual lives would become ineffective.

Keep the fuel in the fire! Stir up the gift that is in you! The oxygen we get from the fire allows us to breathe—the Holy Spirit feeds our spirit to keep the Word flowing in our hearts and minds.

"Feed me, feed me Jesus; Holy Spirit feed me! You are the true and only God—there is none like you!"

"This book of the law shall not depart out of thy mouth; but thou shalt MEDITATE therein day and night, that thou mayest observe to do according to all that is written therein: FOR THEN THOU SHALT MAKE THY WAY PROSPEROUS, AND THEN THOU SHALT HAVE GOOD SUCCESS" (Joshua 1:8, emphasis mine).

27 March ~ "Protect Your Ears"

When flying, most people wear ear plugs, headphones or the mp3/iPod plugs. The purpose is to **protect your ears** and prevent hearing loss during the flight due to the noise inside the aircraft. It is a loud hum at best but is loudest when we're at the highest altitude.

Similarly, we must protect our spiritual ears by shutting out anything that would corrupt our spirit man: illicit music, dirty jokes, and any noise from Satan. We need to protect our ears with spiritual songs and meditate on the Word of God. When we are distracted by the noise of Satan, we make ourselves vulnerable to his tricks and attacks. We want to protect our spiritual ears so we can hear the voice of God and prosper.

"Who hath ears to hear, let him hear. But blessed are your eyes, for they see: and your ears, for they hear" (Matthew 13:9, 16).

28 March ~ "Nothing Compares to the Time I Spend with You"

During my Tallit prayer time tonight, God spoke to me regarding spending time with Him.

All that I've done here and all that I've had to go through to get here was awesome! I've spent a lot of time with the people here on the Compound learning my job—and it has been exciting! I've spent a lifetime in church with the people of God and my family—which has been very comforting!

But, there's nothing like my Tallit time where I get **to spend time with and listen to God**! It was so hard, initially, to get my spirit to be at ease and to rest in order to allow God to minister to me. I have so much I want to say, that it's hard to listen while being silent. My mind wanders and is all over the place. It takes focus, determination and real effort to allow your spirit to rest, relax and ponder while in His presence.

I was supposed to kneel under my Tallit shawl for five minutes—sometimes I was so engrossed in His presence that I went for 10+ minutes.

"Yet the LORD will command his loving kindness in the daytime, and in the night his song shall be with me, and my prayer unto the God of my life" (Psalms 42:8).

"I call to remembrance my song in the night: I commune with mine own heart: and my spirit made diligent search" (Psalms 77:6).

29 March ~ "A Negligent Discharge"

My Force Protection (FP) Officer accidentally discharged his weapon when clearing it upon return from a trip. Thank God, no damage or injuries occurred. An eyewitness told me about it, so I waited for the officer to tell me about the incident, himself. He was a 30-year New York City cop with a vast amount of experience with weapons—of all people to make a mistake like that! When he did come to talk with me about it, his head was down and he was visibly embarrassed by his actions.

I attempted to ease the embarrassment by letting him know that we're all human and make mistakes. I told him to talk to the Commander alone. I then spoke to the Commander who instructed me to prepare a letter of reprimand. I had to do the right thing. My heart was broken because I felt so bad for him, but at least we didn't have to send him home.

As I deliberated the incident and consequences, I came to this conclusion: we all have come short of God's expectations. We have faltered and stumbled. Even "mature" people of God have been tripped by Satan at some point in our walk with God. Why? We are human beings, wrapped in flesh and not immune from faults in life. We have not reached the state of perfection, but we are striving. Even veterans of the Christian faith have been tempted and fell! But God, who is not willing that any should perish, will reach down and brush us off before setting us on a path not to repeat the offense again!

"Thank You, Lord, for Your grace, mercy, long-suffering and forgiveness!" When we, too, like my FP Officer, are strong and experienced and yet still we fail, we are embarrassed by our actions. Repentance is our sole goal to recover from the fault. I thought about the fact that if we don't forgive others' trespasses, our heavenly Father will not forgive ours.

I felt so bad for the officer because it was an irresponsible mistake—he knew the correct procedures, but for some strange reason and in a split second, he pulled the trigger without clearing his round. We're trained not to pull the trigger!

The **negligent discharge** incident could have ruined his career, even though it was a mistake. We, too, make errors called "sin" and we want God to forgive us. We must remember that compassion for the broken and contrite spirit goes a long way. May the light of God shine through me that others will see Jesus and be converted.

I believe the incident happened for a reason—a teachable moment for me and to test my reaction.

"God, You are awesome. Thank You for granting me the wisdom and knowledge of how to handle the situation. You said to ask and You will give what we need, freely."

"If any of you lack wisdom, let him ask of God, that giveth to all men liberally, and upbraideth not; and it shall be given him" (James 1:5).

"But if ye forgive not men their trespasses, neither will your Father forgive your trespasses" (Matthew 6:15).

30 March ~ "Mountains Covered by the Snow"

The cultural advisors took one of the other senior officers and me on a tour of Kabul City. It was fantastic! As we drove closer to the mountains through the streets, I saw houses that looked plastered into the mountains. We went to the top and there were houses with adults, and children running around and playing on the steep rocks. I was amazed that people actually lived in the mountains. Since my arrival, all I'd seen was the **snow covering the mountains**. There was no way I could've imagine that people could survive up there.

Sometimes things are not what they appear to be. We are so small and God is so big that our little minds cannot grasp the awesomeness and power of His glory! He created this earth—*"it is His and the fullness thereof"* (Psalm 24:1). It just blew my mind that it was possible for people to live in the mountains with all that snow. But it is their culture and livelihood.

God has a way of uncovering and revealing the true complexities of things to us in such a simple way.

"Sing, O heavens; and be joyful, O earth; and break forth into singing, O mountains: For the LORD hath comforted his people, and will have mercy upon his afflicted" (Isaiah 49:13).

31 March ~ "What's the Impact"

I tried to list all of the things that I'd accomplished during the cycle for my mid-point performance evaluation. But, I forgot some accomplishments. Some were even more important than the ones I submitted. Nevertheless, God knows what I've accomplished and that is all that matters.

*As an aside: On her birthday today, I thought of my baby girl Kamille. I'm thankful for her accomplishments and encouraged to see the **impact** she has made in the lives of the troubled youth she has had the privilege to serve.*

As I think about judgment day, when we all have to give an account of the deeds done in our bodies, it makes me more vigilant to do more for the Kingdom of God. We must strive to do things that will make an impact for the Kingdom. Thoughtless actions done in vain will not count!

One day, we'll sit at His feet and worship Him for all He's done—oh what joy it will be then!

"For we must all appear before the judgment seat of Christ; that every one may receive the things done in his body, according to that he hath done, whether it be good or bad" (2 Corinthians 5:10).

APRIL 2012

1 April ~ "Spring Cleaning"

As we were cleaning the bunker today, I mopped the floor in the conference room and my workspace. I got the dust and dirt from under the chairs, table and benches. Of course, the mop was quite filthy when I finished.

As we clean our houses and work space, we see the dirt that is removed as we clean. We must also clean our spiritual house. It should be a daily task, not once a year during spring house cleaning.

Put away the old man and put on the new man daily; let go of things that defile the body because God wants our bodies and minds to be pure. Get busy with your daily **"Spring Cleaning!"**

"Purge me with hyssop, and I shall be clean: wash me, and I shall be whiter than snow" (Psalms 51:7).

2 April ~"Dangers Seen and Unseen"

I went to the shooting range today along with the group to zero my weapon. This is a process whereby you fire so many rounds to ensure the sight indicator gives you an accurate shot at the target. While there, the Afghan Police were patrolling the roadway and range area where we were stationed. Just seeing them in their trucks with the high-powered assault rifles atop them was unnerving at times, but they would nod and speak, allowing us to continue to practice.

My prayer for protection from **dangers seen and unseen** has such a different meaning living in this combat zone. We have had a multitude of green on blue incidents—attacks by members of the Afghan police and army against coalition forces in Afghanistan— which have justifiably flooded the news coverage. Some attacks are thought to be an expression of Afghans provoked by the cultural or religious insensitivity of American and North Atlantic Treaty Organization troops. It is only by the grace of God and prayers of the righteous that these folks don't just take us all out as if we were targets on the shooting range.

"The God of my rock; in him will I trust: he is my shield, and the horn of my salvation, my high tower, and my refuge, my saviour; thou savest me from violence. I will call on the LORD, who is worthy to be praised: so shall I be saved from mine enemies" (2 Samuel 22:3-4).

3 April ~ "Be Obedient to the Spirit"

When God speaks to you—you'll know it! When He places someone on your heart so heavy that you can't think of anything else, please **be obedient**! You don't know how much you could be a blessing to someone. Just think someone could miss out on a blessing if you don't heed to the leading of the Spirit.

During my Tallit prayer time, God laid our friends Lisa, Steve and Janelle on my heart. I sent a text to Frank and asked him to give them a financial blessing. I didn't know the specific need at the time, but just knew that they were in need. I found out later that Lisa was diagnosed with an inoperable brain tumor and her husband and daughter have had to spend many hours going back and forth to doctors' appointments and hospital visits.

I do ask God for forgiveness, because I don't always give way to the leading of the Holy Spirit when people are brought to my mind. I'm so, so sorry to anyone who missed out on a blessing, be it word, thought or deed. "God, please supply me, even when I'm not available to be the vessel."

"Cease not to give thanks for you, making mention of you in my prayers; That the God of our Lord Jesus Christ, the Father of glory, may give unto you the spirit of wisdom and revelation in the knowledge of him:" (Ephesians 1:16-17).

"Bear ye one another's burdens, and so fulfil the law of Christ" (Galatians 6:2).

4 April ~ "What's Teachable About Cleaning Dirt Off the Street?"

I went off the Compound with the Communications Technician and the First Sergeant. While riding through the city streets of Kabul, I snapped random pictures of sights I saw, like a man sweeping the dirt on a dirty street. The guys laughed at me, saying, "XO, what are you doing? Why are you taking pictures of a man sweeping dirt? It makes no sense for him to do it, because the street is completely dirty already." I told them that it was a **teachable** moment. Their response was: **"What's teachable about cleaning dirt off the street?"** I did confirm that their question would be added to my book of **teachable** moments. At the time, I didn't respond with a full **teachable** lesson learned, but explained that I normally jot down notes and then ask God to reveal the message to me during my journal time.

The roads we travel here in Kabul are dusty, dirty and, when it rains, muddy! When I see the people walking around in sandals, getting their feet dirty, I remind myself that this lifestyle is the norm for the Afghans. When I witnessed this today, I thought about the Bible days when Jesus walked the dirty, dusty streets of Jerusalem. During the biblical days, there were no paved streets. This was the way of life also for the Israelites. In Kabul it seems worthless to clean or sweep the dust and dirt from the street as it will only get dirty again the same day!

The daily cleaning of the street reduces the amount of dirt that can build up if not swept on a regular basis. It's a process—similar to our cleaning of our minds and refreshing of our spirits daily, only to have Satan to attack again the next day with more dirt. We must sweep and clean every day to ensure we are prepared for the coming of Jesus. We cannot let the sin pile up to a point where it cannot be moved and it has overtaken us permanently.

Daily cleaning of our bodies is necessary. We came from the dust, so we'll continue to be dirty, even after we wash and are then considered clean. We want our minds, hands and hearts to be clean and pure.

So, what's **teachable** about this process? If you don't clean what's dirty, then the dirt will overtake what should be clean.

We live in a filthy world, but we don't have to become filthy. We must purge daily to rid ourselves from fleshly desires and sin. Don't give up and say there's no use in cleaning; keep sweeping. One day, on that great morning, we'll not have to sweep anymore. Instead, we'll be clean with our white robes and crowns of glory to forever be with a loving, pure God in a beautiful, clean city with streets of gold.

"Create in me a clean heart, O God; and renew a right spirit within me" (Psalms 51:10).

"Draw nigh to God, and he will draw nigh to you. Cleanse your hands, ye sinners; and purify your hearts, ye double minded" (James 4:8).

"And be not conformed to this world: but be ye transformed by the renewing of your mind, that ye may prove what is that good, and acceptable, and perfect, will of God" (Romans 12:2).

4 April ~ "Combat Zone Tourist"

My Communications Technician told me I was acting like a **tourist in a combat zone**, and that wasn't good! He said I was snapping pictures and not giving heed to the dangers of my surroundings. Actually, I was being very careful and discrete about my picture taking, but he couldn't see that—I was sitting behind him.

In this life, we must be mindful that we don't become a targeted tourist! Satan is real and his prime mission is to steal, kill and destroy. He is roaming, seeking whom he may devour. We can't walk around with our heads in the air checking out the scenery, being engulfed in the pleasures of life and in this world.

We must be vigilant and aware of Satan's traps and devices. Yes, God's creations are picturesque and a wonder to behold, but the evil spirit is ugly and dangerous. Don't be uninformed and naïve; be watchful. Don't act like a tourist during your spiritual warfare!

"Therefore let us not sleep, as do others; but let us watch and be sober" (1 Thessalonians 5:6).

5 April ~ "The Babysitter"

Gee, babysitting these folks is a full time job! Someone did tell me that I would do a lot of babysitting while deployed. Oh well, I'm a mother and accustomed to tending to issues and I have mastered conflict resolution as well.

I had to deal with my "Type A" soul today. Diffusing what could have been an explosion, I pray constantly for peace, especially behind the wire.

Today I have confirmed my learning that babysitting adults is a quality of leadership that must be attained in order to be successful!

A soft word diffuses anger!

"A soft answer turneth away wrath: but grievous words stir up anger" (Proverbs 15:1).

6 April ~ "Riding with a Grenade in My Hand"

Why was I holding a grenade in my hand while riding to one of our other sites? The grenade is an explosive device that my Senior Logistician admonished me to respect. Many have lost lives and limbs by disrespecting it or playing with it. "It is not a toy—this is considered part of our armor and is meant to do a lot of damage against the enemy," warned my Senior Logistician.

We were on our way to the armory to dispose of old weapons that were no longer needed at our Compound. Someone had to hold the grenade because some smart person was playing with it and broke the pin. I had to hold it to keep the pin in place until we reached the armory disposal lot. My arm was so stiff when I arrived because my whole body was tensed with anxiety during the bumpy ride.

In the same way, the devil and his toys are nothing to play with. Playing with sin is like playing with a grenade. It can go off and destroy you and those around you. You can dabble in sin and wrongdoing for a while, but the accumulative effect will eventually produce an explosion.

A foul tongue is a grenade as well, waiting to explode. It only takes a tug at the pin and we get ticked off and explode with our tongues.

Don't **hold onto the grenade**—let it go and get rid of it properly. Command it to go to the pit of hell so it won't harm others.

"I said, I will take heed to my ways, that I sin not with my tongue: I will keep my mouth with a bridle, while the wicked is before me" (Psalms 39:1).

"But the tongue can no man tame; it is an unruly evil, full of deadly poison" (James 3:8).

7 April ~ "Receiving Godly Counsel"

The psychologists from my Washington Headquarters came today to talk with and counsel employees who felt the need. Most did not feel the need to talk, which was fine with the psychologists. These visitors were also on orders to talk to me about the Vehicle Borne Improvised Explosive Device incident that took place March 22nd. I told them that I had neither negative flashbacks nor issues with sleeping. I told them that my life is in God's hands and I have neither fear nor worry. By the time I was finished with them, they were hyped and encouraged!

I had an opportunity to minister to and encourage one of the Reports Officers (RO). She was having a tough time with her supervisor who had an EXTREME TYPE A personality! She was a believer and felt it was just a test of her faith and trust in God.

When God puts someone in your path to counsel you and guide you into truth, receive the assignment, appreciate the person and thank God. We never know when someone is going through hard times and trials and just needs someone to talk to and confide in. When led by God, be on the giving end of counseling, mostly by listening and responding only when God sends a message your way.

Just as we have earthly counselors who attempt to bring our feelings out, we have a heavenly Father who guides and directs our steps when we are confused, unsure or downhearted. He loves us so much that He'll send us to the right person or send that person to us just when we need them the most.

Even though we may think we're spiritually strong, when God leads us, we should receive the godly counseling knowing that God meant it for our good!

"The ear that heareth the reproof of life abideth among the wise. He that refuseth instruction despiseth his own soul: but he that heareth reproof getteth understanding. The fear of the LORD is the instruction of wisdom; and before honour is humility" (Proverbs 15:31-33).

8 April ~"Easter Service: Afghanistan Style"

Last night, I prepped for communion and Easter Service held today. This was the first Easter Service ever held on this Compound in Afghanistan. I asked God to bless the Commander who gave us permission to have this service and have a Bible Study. We utilized non-alcoholic red grape juice and Afghan "toe bread." The Pastor (one of the senior officers) conducted the service and the RO and I assisted with serving communion. It was astonishing! One participant stated, "I've never had communion out of a creamer cup before." We were being creative.

The message title was: "The Resurrection."

"Martha saith unto him, I know that he shall rise again in the resurrection at the last day. Jesus said unto her, I am the resurrection, and the life: he that believeth in me, though he were dead, yet shall he live: And whosoever liveth and believeth in me shall never die. Believest thou this? She saith unto him, Yea, Lord: I believe that thou art the Christ, the Son of God, which should come into the world" (John 11:24-27).

The Pastor mentioned during his Easter sermon that he deletes songs from his library that say, "I should have been on the cross instead of Jesus." That comment flared up a lesson in my spirit.

It took a special vessel ordained by God—His only begotten Son. He was the only one that could do the job that no other man could do! If it was any of us, we would have said "no way Lord God" just as we do now when we're asked to do something for Him. If it wasn't for Jesus dying on that Cross, we would be forever lost!

No other person could've taken His place on Calvary. We understand that Jesus didn't deserve to die for our sins, but He loved us so much that He did it anyway. He was able to bear it because His Father gave Him the strength and the will to suffer that horrible, painful death.

What love it is when a man will lay down his life for his friends. We serve an awesome God. The Trinity—God the Father, Son and Holy Ghost are one! "Lord, I Believe! I believe in the Trinity. I believe only Jesus could do the job. I believe He died, rose and is now on the right hand of God making intersession just for me." He did it, even if it had been just for me. And I'm grateful and reverence His mighty acts towards me.

Jesus was the only one who—not necessarily should— could be on that Cross. It was all a part of God's plan to bring us back into a relationship with Him. "Thank You Jesus, for dying on that cross for ME!"

"For it is not possible that the blood of bulls and of goats should take away sins. Wherefore when he cometh into the world, he saith, Sacrifice and offering thou wouldest not, but a body hast thou prepared me:" (Hebrews 10:4-5).

9 April ~ "The Howl of a Cat"

The house cats roam about here daily looking for food. We've been told not to feed them so they will take care of the rodents, snakes and other prey. But in the winter and spring, the game is almost non-existent.

There will come a time in our lives when there will be "a famine in the land" (v.11), where we will look for the Word of God and won't be able to find it. We will be like the house cats, howling for food! When we can eat off the fat of the land, we should store up as much as possible. We must understand that the famine will come. We don't want to be "so smart" and complacent to think that the well water will always be there.

Don't be in a situation where you'll have to starve, walking around howling like a cat. Eat the Word daily!

"Behold, the days come, saith the Lord GOD, that I will send a famine in the land, not a famine of bread, nor a thirst for water, but of hearing the words of the LORD: And they shall wander from sea to sea, and from the north even to the east, they shall run to and fro to seek the word of the LORD, and shall not find it" (Amos 8:11-12).

"Blessed are they which do hunger and thirst after righteousness: for they shall be filled" (Matthew 5:6).

9 April ~ "Trusting Relationship"

While sitting in the sun catching some rays, I thought about the fact that we have Afghan guards with guns protecting our Compound. With the recent "green on blue" attacks, we can only wonder if our trust in them is solid. Yet, it pays to be courteous and respectful. Gifts of treats and special food are often offered as a demonstration of our appreciation for the work they do. We may never know who is affiliated with the Taliban to infiltrate our spaces and attack, but the power of God's love and protection is more powerful than Satan's desire to kill, steal and destroy.

It behooves us as U.S. Government employees to maintain that **trusting relationship**; because we are on their territory and at their mercy sometimes. Even if Satan planted someone here, greater is He that is in me than he that is in this world. "My trust is not in man, but in You, God, who is the ultimate guard and protector of my life." I have a solid, **trusting relationship** with my God!

"But mine eyes are unto thee, O God the Lord: in thee is my trust; leave not my soul destitute. Keep me from the snares which they have laid for me, and

the gins of the workers of iniquity. Let the wicked fall into their own nets, whilst that I withal escape" (Psalms 148:8-10).

9 April ~ "When There is No Shade"

While sitting in the lounge chair on the front yard inside of the Compound, I was enjoying the sun's rays. Then, the clouds covered the sun and a feeling of coolness came about. The sun can be brutal to our skin, eyes, etc. If there is no protection from the sun, damage can occur. When the rays of sunshine are so forcefully beaming down on us, we seek shelter and shade to protect us.

Similarly, **when there is no shade** from the forces of life, we look to God for relief, for covering and shelter. He will shield us with a cloud of mercy to protect us—but we must *seek* the shelter.

"And the LORD will create upon every dwelling place of mount Zion, and upon her assemblies, a cloud and smoke by day, and the shining of a flaming fire by night: for upon all the glory shall be a defence. And there shall be a tabernacle for a shadow in the daytime from the heat, and for a place of refuge, and for a covert from storm and from rain" (Isaiah 4:5-6).

10 April ~ "This is Not Our Home"

Earth is not our home; we're just passing through. We're only here for a temporary time period in order to fulfill His purpose and then receive our eternal heavenly home. I had a dynamic discussion with our Lead Mechanic about our temporary assignment here in Afghanistan. Therefore, since Afghanistan **is not our home**, but only a temporary assignment, we should not get comfortable here. This was difficult—I feel I need to spend much more time here. Yet, we're just passing through. We must complete our mission and go home!

God has a place prepared for those of us who are in Christ Jesus. We must wear our tenure here loosely and not hold tight to those things that are temporal.

"In my Father's house are many mansions: if it were not so, I would have told you. I go to prepare a place for you. And if I go and prepare a place for

you, I will come again, and receive you unto myself; that where I am, there ye may be also" (John 14:2-3).

10 April ~ "The Way of Escape"

Today our 1SGT (First Sergeant) and two Admin Officers were involved in an accident where the driver hit an Afghan woman who had to go to the hospital. The people gathered into a mob around the vehicle, shouting and banging on their up-armored vehicle. When things were about to get totally out of control and their safety was at risk, one Afghan Policeman stabbed the tire which made a loud noise! The crowd dispersed and 1SGT directed the driver to speed away! My heart went out to the driver—he was driving aggressively and it was the first time he has ever struck someone with a vehicle. At home in the U.S., this would be considered a hit and run! But out here, you better run to save your life and those of your passengers.

This incident reminded me of the scripture which speaks about God giving us a way out of temptation and a **way of escape** from the enemy. Sometimes we can get mobbed by Satan's attacks; our defenses are up and we're ready to shoot at anything! We can be surrounded by trouble on every side, with no **way of escape** in sight.

Then God, pouring out His grace and mercy, will make a **way of escape** from the trouble. The prayers of the righteous availeth much as we escape to safety.

"There hath no temptation taken you but such as is common to man: but God is faithful, who will not suffer you to be tempted above that ye are able; but will with the temptation also make a way to escape, that ye may be able to bear it" (1 Corinthians 10:13).

"Watch ye therefore, and pray always, that ye may be accounted worthy to escape all these things that shall come to pass, and to stand before the Son of man" (Luke 21:36).

11 April ~ "The Gift of Shoes"

Today we visited the Afghan Women's Education Center (AWEC). Members at the Compound partnered with this non-profit organization which provides assistance to women and children. We collected funds to purchase over 420 pairs of shoes. This school is specifically structured to meet the needs of "street children." These children must work to support their families and cannot attend regular school. These children don't have many of the things we take for granted. Some don't have shoes and their clothes are dirty, torn and ragged.

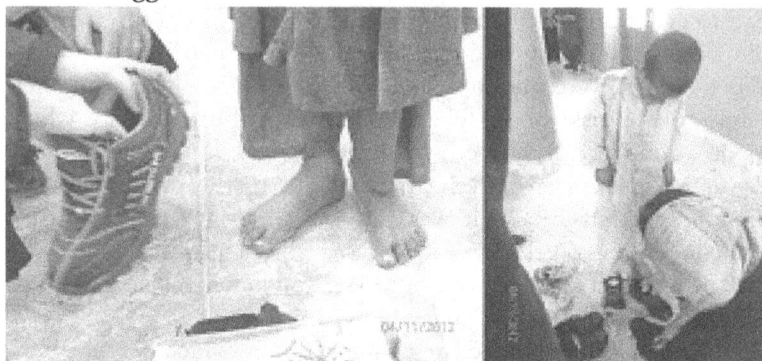

Being a part of this mission was so humbling and heartwarming. The children were very grateful and respectful when waiting in line to get their shoes. It made my heart rejoice to see members of our staff enjoy giving to and helping these children. It made me really feel like God sent me here to serve and make a difference for these people. I can't do everything, but I can do something.

I couldn't help but think of Christ washing the disciples' feet. Peter didn't feel worthy and didn't want Jesus to wash his feet. Jesus warned Peter that if he refused to get his feet washed then he could not associate with Him. It was then that Peter complied and wanted to get both his hands and head washed. (John 13:4-9).

These children received a **gift of shoes**—their feet were dirty and some diseased. I humbled myself (because, as Frank knows, I don't touch feet!) to actually assist some of them with putting on the shoes, touching their feet in the process. But the joy on their little faces when they tried them on and the shoes fit was priceless!

I remembered when we had conducted foot washings at church. We practiced this act of humility during special Ten-Day Fasting services held on a quarterly basis. During one service, we had to wash Sister Grace's (one of our senior church members) feet and I almost had a tantrum when we had to do it. I eventually humbled myself and submitted to the will of God in service to others. I recalled when my niece, Alisha, washed her first set of feet and when I coached my other niece, LaVira, to wash other members' feet; both also learned to humble themselves.

In order for us to be in Christ and a part of His Kingdom, we must humble ourselves as He did, even to the point of washing/touching someone's dirty feet to help them. It is not about the dirty feet and getting our hands dirty, it is about being humbled enough to care about someone other than yourself. It is about giving and helping even when it's not convenient. God wants us to learn that lesson of humility—one day we'll need someone to show compassion to us.

"He riseth from supper, and laid aside his garments; and took a towel, and girded himself. After that he poureth water into a bason, and began to wash the disciples' feet, and to wipe them with the towel wherewith he was girded. Then cometh he to Simon Peter: and Peter saith unto him, Lord, dost thou wash my feet? Jesus answered and said unto him, What I do thou knowest not now; but thou shalt know hereafter. Peter saith unto him, Thou shalt never wash my feet. Jesus answered him, If I wash thee not, thou hast no part with me. Simon Peter saith unto him, Lord, not my feet only, but also my hands and my head" (John 13:4-9).

12 April ~ "I WON!"

We had our Compound Idol Game tonight! My team members forced me to participate even though I was the organizer, so I practiced one of my mother's favorite songs, "Give Me a Clean Heart"[2] by Margaret Douroux.

Singing without music is challenging when you're not a singer, but I wanted the audience to focus on the words. I wanted hearts to be uplifted and God to be glorified!

I believe God was pleased…and **I won**—not only the competition, but also a few hearts. The prize was a coupon for a *free massage*. I gave it to one of the Reports Officers who needed it more than I did.

---

[2] Dr. Margaret J. Douroux. *Give Me a Clean Heart* © 1970 Earl Pleasant Publishing.

"And I, if I be lifted up from the earth, will draw all men unto me" (John 12:32).

"O come, let us sing unto the Lord: let us make a joyful noise to the rock of our salvation" (Psalm 95:1)

13 April ~ "The Lasting Brand"

Today I was watching a TV show about a lady talking about her successful business with branding products. What is a brand? It is a mark to identify something. A lasting brand, a brand that lasts for years, will be most successful.

If you want to be successful, get in with the **brand that is lasting**. The Jesus Brand is one that will outlast any other brand. It will last throughout eternity. Put the Jesus Brand on everything you do. There is another brand that we do not want to be associated with: the mark of the beast from Revelation. Accept the free gift of the Jesus Brand and be true to it daily. Don't frustrate or deface it by living in such a way to bring dishonor or shame to the Jesus Brand.

"But ye [are] a chosen generation, a royal priesthood, an holy nation, a peculiar people; that ye should shew forth the praises of him who hath called you out of darkness into his marvellous light;" (1 Peter 2:9).

"Labour not for the meat which perisheth, but for that meat which endureth unto everlasting life, which the Son of man shall give unto you: for him hath God the Father sealed" (John 6:27).

13 April ~ "Unappreciated in Your Own Country"

Occasionally, the hard work you do is not appreciated at home. Being away from family and friends has made it a difficult time in my life, but I asked God to prepare me to be able to fulfill this mission. I've tried to stay focused on my new tasks, new challenges and my personal mission to reach new people.

I don't see myself as outgoing or sociable—I've worked extra hard to become that in Afghanistan. As a leader, I must lead by example! I did lead by example at home, but sometimes I felt

unappreciated. Often, I felt that I was taken for granted…not that I wanted accolades or praise, but I wanted my best products to be used to benefit the task, the cause or the mission.

Every now and then, you have to get away from all that you know and become quiet so you can hear the voice of God. Several scriptures in the New Testament mention *"[n]o prophet is accepted in his **own country**"* (Luke 4:24). I feel this deployment is part of the plan to grow, mold and shape me more into the person God wants me to be.

I do feel appreciated by my boss and subordinates. I've seen God work miracles here on the Compound. I pray daily for protection over this Compound and its occupants. I really feel like I'm making a difference here in Afghanistan. Participating with the shoe ministry at AWEC (Afghan Women's Education Center) was so humbling and fulfilling as a member of the Body of Christ.

When I return, I will bring to my **own country** the things God poured into me while away in a foreign country.

"And they were offended in him. But Jesus said unto them, A prophet is not without honour, save in his own country, and in his own house" (Matthew 13:57).

14 April ~ "I Apologize"

Two hard words to say, but easy to digest—**I apologize**! *"A man's belly shall be satisfied with the fruit of his mouth; and with the increase of his lips shall he be filled. Death and life are in the power of the tongue: and they that love it shall eat the fruit thereof"* (Proverb 18:20-21).

I had a discussion with one of the senior officers today about someone who wanted to come to discuss a mutual initiative. The officer was a little rough in pressing me for what I wanted her to do and I could only tell her to be available. She seemed frustrated and short-tempered.

Later she came to my desk and **apologized**. I accepted. She said I was very patient with her and she should not have talked to me the way she did. I wasn't upset nor did I feel bothered by her earlier comments. Instead, I used this moment to let God teach me something.

I remember the remorse I felt when an apology from me was in order when I had an altercation with one of my peers; and, even more so when I expressed regret to my Commander for not informing him of an incident that happened on the Compound. These incidents caused me to acknowledge my sin and confess to God for repentance.

How often do we **apologize** or say, "I'm sorry" and *really mean it*? Too often we give lip service to appease someone, but don't really care in our hearts. We quickly say whatever we need to say to move on. God wants us to have a repentant heart and mindset. Get off the high horse and be humble enough to say—I was wrong—**I apologize**! It is okay to say it and mean it.

"Forbearing one another, and forgiving one another, if any man have a quarrel against any: even as Christ forgave you, so also do ye" (Colossians 3:13).

15 April ~ "Get Off the Roof"

Today is my only son, T.J.'s birthday. My Communications Technician is close to his age; therefore, I look at him as my son. Both are in the computer technician field and both are very intelligent and experts in their fields. While my Communications Technician and I were on the roof today checking materials needed for the communications satellite, I mentioned my son T.J. and that it was his birthday. It was a beautiful sunny day. We suddenly heard popping sounds as we looked over the ledge. When we heard more, we came to the conclusion that they were small arms fire and that we should **get off the roof** and get to the bunker. Once we got to the bunker, the security alarms went off. There was an attack with small arms fire at a nearby installation.

Though we were not the target, nor were any shots fired near the roof, we could have been in the wrong place at the wrong time if shots had made their way to our rooftop. Being on the roof did put us in a position to be fired upon if they saw us.

When you put yourself in a position where the devil can take shots at you, you are in complete danger. When you live a lifestyle that is unpleasing to God, you are in complete danger. Sometimes people stay in danger because they feel there's no hope and things will not change for them. **Get off the roof** of sin and receive salvation from the one who loves and cares for you and your safety.

"He that diligently seeketh good procureth favour: but he that seeketh mischief, it shall come unto him" (Proverbs 11:27).

15 April ~ "The Fight Within"

While we were on lockdown due to insurgent attacks and fighting outside our Compound, two of our leaders were involved in an altercation within the bunker. There should be peace on the inside—comfort, safety and oneness. Yet, the two leaders almost went to blows with each other while the *real* fighting was going on outside. They had a simple disagreement which escalated to chest bumping, yelling and cursing at one another. The male leader was so angry that he put a hole in the door with his fist!

We must be careful of the devices of the enemy to get us to fight amongst ourselves. Flesh and pride cause us to war against one another. We can become very distracted regarding our real enemy. Once we are distracted, it is easy for the enemy to trip and trick us. Pride and self-exaltation will bring about friction when confrontation occurs. We should remain focused on our call and ministry—especially as leaders—because others are watching; therefore, let your words be few. Christians often become stumbling blocks for unbelievers when we behave in such a way that is not becoming of a godly posture. Churches often have discord and fighting within their congregations. Again, this causes the unbelievers to discount and distrust the Christian walk. As the Body of Christ, seek first to alleviate and deflate confrontations to avoid **"the fight within."**

"Be not rash with thy mouth, and let not thine heart be hasty to utter any thing before God: for God is in heaven, and thou upon earth: therefore let thy words be few" (Ecclesiastes 5:2).

16 April ~ "Someone's Knocking"

I woke up to someone knocking on my door. It was the First Sergeant letting me know that I overslept and missed the morning brief. Thank God I heard the knock and was able to get up! Like Sister Miriam Macey from my home church has testified: "It's a blessing to wake up and a bonus to get up." Not everyone that wakes up can get out of the bed. God has blessed me with yet another opportunity to see a brand new day. I will *"rejoice and be glad in it"* (Psalm 118:24). I am thanking God that I heard the knock on the spiritual door to my heart. I opened it and invited Him to come in and dwell in me.

It was a busy day that reinforced the notion that I love my job!

"Behold, I stand at the door, and knock: if any man hear my voice, and open the door, I will come in to him, and will sup with him, and he with me" (Revelations 3:20).

17 April ~ "The Watchmen"

I had Command Quarters (CQ) in the Technical Operations Command (TOC) tonight on the 1900 hours to 0700 hours shift. This task calls for the person to oversee the safety of the Compound on night duty. This includes monitoring 18 cameras, controlling ingress and egress, communicating with guards over the radio, checking three guard gates, walking the perimeter, starting and shutting down each vehicle, checking the alarms, accounting for all the property, checking each rally station (ensuring the communications are present and working properly), ensuring everyone is in for the night and accounted for, and texting the Commander to let him know all accounted for.

As I viewed the camera, watching for any unusual activity, I thought about the scripture which referred to **the watchmen** on the wall looking over the city. We also have guard forces that watch 24/7.

God provides watchmen for us to ensure the safety of His people. He gives us pastors, teachers, and other **watchmen** to care for our souls. These **watchmen** must be vigilant to warn us when we are in danger or disobedient. **The watchmen's** job is to sound the horn and make a warning cry that those who hear are saved. Thank God our **watchmen** are on duty 24/7. There's no room for sleeping on the job.

"Son of man, I have made thee a watchman unto the house of Israel: therefore hear the word at my mouth, and give them warning from me. When I say unto the wicked, Thou shalt surely die; and thou givest him not warning,

nor speakest to warn the wicked from his wicked way, to save his life; the same wicked man shall die in his iniquity; but his blood will I require at thine hand. Yet if thou warn the wicked, and he turn not from his wickedness, nor from his wicked way, he shall die in his iniquity; but thou hast delivered thy soul" (Ezekiel 3:17-19).

"I have set watchmen upon thy walls, O Jerusalem, [which] shall never hold their peace day nor night: ye that make mention of the LORD, keep not silence," (Isaiah 62:6).

18 April ~ "The Dawning of a New Day"

While ending my 1900 hours to 0700 hours shift on Command Quarters (CQ), I watched the sun rise on the security cameras. I watched night segue into dawn. Dawn is dim and day is sunlight. That gradual process from night to dawn to daylight is awesome to watch as it happens! We see in our lives where we've experienced darkness and God brought us to the light of a **New Day**. There is no more crying about yesterday. You can't bring it back—it is gone forever, never to show its appearance again!

God gives us a **New Day** every day (as my father would always say in his prayer, "a day that we have never seen before and will never see again"). Then, just to make it even better, God gives us new mercies daily. *"Great is thy faithfulness"* (v.23).

"It is of the Lord's mercies that we are not consumed, because his compassions fail not. They are new every morning: great is thy faithfulness" (Lamentations 3:22-23).

Your **dawning of a New Day** is faithful. Take each day as it comes and live it to the fullest and to His glory! Be thankful and bless His name.

"Enter into his gates with thanksgiving, and into his courts with praise: be thankful unto him, and bless his name. For the LORD is good; his mercy is everlasting; and his truth endureth to all generations" (Psalms 100:4-5).

19 April ~ "The Word of the Day"

Each morning, we receive a threat briefing and I provide the administrative movements and announcements. The **word of the day** is given to everyone in the Afghanistan Theater. Knowing the word given is important to your—and others'—safety and wellbeing.

I thank God for my knowing and understanding the code word of EVERYDAY—Jesus! No other name but Jesus! When we are in trouble, we can call out the name JESUS!

Jesus knows who are; you must acknowledge the word to get in. Just believe in your heart that Jesus died for your sins; repent and confess your sins. He is willing to receive you. What a comforting feeling to know if you get in trouble, you have the code word you can use EVERYDAY—JESUS!

"My sheep hear my voice, and I know them, and they follow me:" (John 10:27).

20 April ~ "I'm Fired?"

I had to prepare a memorandum for the record regarding the poor performance of one of my contractor staff. My prayer was that he would find a job where he could contribute.

On this job, everyone is required to pull their own weight and do their job. If you don't—go home! It may sound harsh, but it is unfair that taxpayers' money is being spent on non-performers. What a waste!

So is it in the Body of Christ; we must bear our own cross and pull our own weight. If we don't live up to our task to show love and point people to Jesus, then we are wasting our time. God has given us time to give Him the honor and glory. That time should be utilized to build up the kingdom. Proverbs speaks about the sluggard and those who refuse to work.

If you don't multiply what God has given you, then you can lose it to someone else who can do something with it. **You're Fired!**

"The soul of the sluggard desireth, and hath nothing: but the soul of the diligent shall be made fat" (Proverbs 13: 4).

April ~20 "The Oversized Truck"

One vehicle got separated from the convoy returning from one of our detachments 45 minutes away. One mechanic and a gunner were almost to the Compound when they were turned away at a Kabul checkpoint due to the size of the truck. We went on high alert because the communications equipment was spotty. We had one officer in the Technical Operations Command (TOC) trying to direct them (via radio and cell phone) to a more secure route using her oversized map of Kabul city.

Finally, upon arrival we discovered that the big truck that they drove back from the other detachment was too tall to fit under the gate to the Compound. The mechanics had to cut the top rails twice before they could finally drive it in. This process was unnerving because we did not want to draw attention to our efforts by the surrounding neighbors.

There are times in our lives where we must cut off some things so we can fit into the mold where God wants us to be. If we are high-minded (**oversized** head), we need to eliminate the pride so our head will fit through the door. During the process of trimming the unwanted unrighteousness from our spiritual lives, there should be some signs that we are decreasing as God increases in our lives.

"He must increase, but I must decrease" (John 3:30).

21 April ~ "The Enemy is Quiet When it Rains"

Today during my morning briefing, the words for the day were: Let it rain! You see, **the enemy is quiet when it rains**.

Just as the enemy in this country tends to reduce the number of attacks during rain or snow, so does the enemy of our souls. When the Holy Spirit is raining down on us, Satan can't do a thing but stay quiet. That's why it is awesome to be in the presence of the Lord under the showers of the Holy Spirit as He pours down as rain upon us.

"Be glad then, ye children of Zion, and rejoice in the LORD your God: for he hath given you the former rain moderately, and he will cause to come down for you the rain, the former rain, and the latter rain in the first month" (Joel 2:23).

22 April ~ "Without Instructions"

Being on this small Compound with nowhere to go for recreation except the small gym could cause some to become claustrophobic. I asked the Commander if we could purchase a ping pong table and pool table to help foster cohesiveness and recreation. He checked with the leadership in DC and received approval by email.

We received the pool and ping pong tables today! The setup for both tables was by sight and experience. You see, the equipment came with no instructions. When you purchase equipment in the U.S., it comes with instructions and, sometimes, an installer. But, here in Afghanistan, you get what you get and sometimes not all of what you paid for. There were screws and pieces everywhere; it looked like a disaster and my heart was weary. But with a lot of effort, experience and teamwork, the guys got them both up and functioning!

Some accomplishments we made in life came with **no instructions**. But God guided us to where we needed to be to enable us to be successful. I thought about how I am a wife, mother, and grandmother. There were **no instructions** that came with these life experiences, but the encouragement, support and love of family and friends helped me to develop into these roles.

God gives us His Word as our guide and instruction to righteous living. Thank God He did not leave us alone without instructions in how to maneuver throughout our spiritual walk.

"All scripture is given by inspiration of God, and is profitable for doctrine, for reproof, for correction, for instruction in righteousness: That the man of God may be perfect, thoroughly furnished unto all good works" (2 Timothy 3:16-17).

22 April ~ "Mellowing...Who, Me?"

I'm not a softy, but I have **mellowed** over the last 10 years. In the office, we were teasing each other about being soft and giving in. I stated that yes; I've **mellowed** over the years. I do remember a time in my life that I'd let no one get over on me. Revenge was mine! Forgiveness was not my cup of tea. But God, who is loving, caring, patient, and long-suffering worked with me until I mellowed to His liking. It is a process!

When I look back on all of the times that I was bull-headed, I can only drop my head in shame. But the God who forgives has forgiven me of my past and I can now move forward with my head up and with confidence knowing how I should treat others.

"And when ye stand praying, forgive, if ye have ought against any: that your Father also which is in heaven may forgive you your trespasses. But if ye do not forgive, neither will your Father which is in heaven forgive your trespasses" (Mark 11:25-26).

23 April ~"The Mixture"

Today was a mixture of sun and rain. In life, we're going to have both sunny and rainy days. They each have their purpose and fulfillment. In Christ, we also experience tough times and glorious high times. God's sun shines and His rain falls on the believer and unbeliever alike. We take what God gives us as nourishment for our souls. *"That ye may be the children of your Father which is in heaven: for he maketh his sun to rise on the evil and on the good, and sendeth rain on the just and on the unjust"* (Matthew 5:45).

We can't always be on the mountain top with everything going our way. We will suffer disappointment, heartache and pain. He promised that it won't always be dim and gloomy. Be thankful and patient, even during the cloudy and rainy days. They have a profound purpose that allows us to grow and teaches us to appreciate and be content with whatever state we find ourselves in.

"Not that I speak in respect of want: for I have learned, in whatsoever state I am, therewith to be content" (Philippians 4:11).

24 April ~ "What— My Name Is Not On the List?"

Today we went to another Compound that was about 10 minutes away. We went to take the required mail handler's training. We completed and submitted our paperwork for the class three weeks prior. Much to our dismay, the instructor made a roll call and our names were not on the list. The First Sergeant immediately got hot-headed, shouting about how we sent our paperwork in weeks ago and that someone didn't do their job in updating the roster.

Surprisingly, I remained calm. Keeping my composure, I firmly informed the instructor that we were dropped off for this class and would not reschedule because we planned to successfully complete the class on this day.

The instructor finally gave in and let us remain in the class. He actually was very helpful with the instruction and exam. Thank God for grace—a calm spirit is always best every time!

There was much anger, discouragement and disappointment when we heard those words: **"Your Names are Not on the List!"** Just think, in the Day of Judgment—if you have not lived your life pleasing to God—He will say: *"Depart from me, I know you not."* What a sad, depressing and terrifying day to hear that your name is not written in the Lamb's Book of Life! "Lord, please prepare me to be pure and holy, tried and true. In so doing, **my name will be on the list!**"

Even as a strong believer, I learned a lot from this moment today. It gave me more vigor to do the right thing and mind my tongue and thoughts so I will be accepted by the Almighty God.

"Strive to enter in at the strait gate: for many, I say unto you, will seek to enter in, and shall not be able. When once the master of the house is risen up, and hath shut to the door, and ye begin to stand without, and to knock at the door, saying, Lord, Lord, open unto us; and he shall answer and say unto you, I know you not whence ye are: Then shall ye begin to say, We have eaten and drunk in thy presence, and thou hast taught in our streets. But he shall say, I tell you, I know you not whence ye are; depart from me, all ye workers of iniquity" (Luke 13:24-27).

24 April ~ "Successful Kingdom Building"

We all want to be successful in our jobs, relationships, etc. I was sharing with my son, T.J., by text what he should pray for when seeking a new job: "that his skills and abilities will bring glory to God and further the development of the organization." That's true success!

When you bring glory to God and let your light shine, men will see your good work ethic and want some of what you have—giving God the glory. Just think of a boss who would say: "Thank God for such a great, hard worker. I'll make him successful in my company as he has furthered the development of my organization." Success!

We, too, can bring success to the field of souls—**kingdom building**. We must strive to live so that people will see Christ in our lives and turn to Him with a repentant heart. Adding souls to the fold is **"Successful Kingdom Building!"**

"Now therefore ye are no more strangers and foreigners, but fellowcitizens with the saints, and of the household of God; And are built upon the foundation of the apostles and prophets, Jesus Christ himself being the chief corner stone; In whom all the building fitly framed together groweth unto an holy temple in the Lord: In whom ye also are builded together for an habitation of God through the Spirit" (Ephesians 2:19-22).

25 April ~ "Great Bible Study"

We had a really great Bible study lesson tonight on spiritual gifts. We had more attendees to join us. The Pastor and I shared our prayer and desire for God to send others after us to continue the Bible study and other mission services.

The fact that this Compound never had a structured Bible study service was humbling. I was afraid at first, but God gave me the courage to approach the Commander and received approval.

My lesson: when God gives you something to do, be confident and move forward!

Each time we had Bible study, I received encouragement and strength to go on. Even though it was not about me or intended specifically for me, I benefited from what God allowed to happen on this Compound. "Thank You Lord!"

"But continue thou in the things which thou hast learned and hast been assured of, knowing of whom thou hast learned [them]; All scripture [is] given by inspiration of God, and [is] profitable for doctrine, for reproof, for correction, for instruction in righteousness:" (2 Timothy 3:14,16).

26 April ~ "The Hard Head"

Today I was waiting on God to give me the right words to say to a staff member about his unprofessional behavior. It saddens me to see our young men destroy their lives due to Satan's power over them.

When you hear the term "he's hard-headed", it means that he won't listen and learn. Stubbornness is another term used. You can continue to be bull-headed if you want, but sooner or later, you could lose everything as quickly as you lose your temper.

A **hard head** brings on headaches. As a child, I was told that a **hard head** makes a soft bottom.

Don't put yourself in the predicament to receive chastisement from God. He will not put up with our stubbornness forever. There is a limit. Don't press God to the limit. Repent and do the right thing!

"...To day if ye will hear his voice, Harden not your heart, as in the provocation, and as in the day of temptation in the wilderness: When your fathers tempted me, proved me, and saw my work. Forty years long was I grieved with this generation, and said, It is a people that do err in their heart, and they have not known my ways: Unto whom I sware in my wrath that they should not enter into my rest" (Psalms 95:7b-11).

27 April ~ "Be Accountable"

Today I had a stimulating discussion with my Senior Logistician and one of the Reports Officers about accountability. We talked about how some employees perform at 120% and others only put in 60%. We talked about the importance of everyone contributing to the fullest while deployed to make the load more manageable for all. When I think about how we put in more time and energy and no one really cares or notices, it is okay—we work for God, not man! We must **be accountable** to God for what we do, say, and how we react to frustrations and wrongdoings. It can be frustrating to see so-called Christians half-stepping and still professing. They still get blessed, come and go as they please in worship services, but still claim victory.

Those incidents should push us closer to God. Focusing on what others do and don't do can cause us to waiver or fall. Therefore, keep your eyes on Jesus. Remember He is the only Judge and we must **be accountable** to Him. In the Day of Judgment, we will all stand before God ALONE.

Don't wait - **be accountable** today!

"For it is written, As I live, saith the Lord, every knee shall bow to me, and every tongue shall confess to God. So then every one of us shall give account of himself to God. Let us not therefore judge one another any more: but judge this rather, that no man put a stumblingblock or an occasion to fall in his brother's way" (Romans 14:11-13).

28 April ~ "Finding the Calm in the Combat Zone"

Another beautiful day in Afghanistan! While enjoying the warm sun and nice breeze, God dropped this in my spirit.

When all hell is breaking loose on the ground, fighting, sniper gun fire, explosions, Vehicle Borne Improvised Explosive Devices (VBIEDS), etc.—we can find peace and calm by looking up. Life can be so turbulent that we cannot see our way through. Don't despair; God is right there, waiting to bring the **calm** in the midst of your storm. These scripture have been my comfort and shield.

"I will lift up mine eyes unto the hills, from whence cometh my help. My help cometh from the LORD, which made heaven and earth. He will not suffer thy foot to be moved: he that keepeth thee will not slumber. Behold, he that keepeth Israel shall neither slumber nor sleep. The LORD is thy keeper: the LORD is thy shade upon thy right hand. The sun shall not smite thee by day, nor the moon by night. The Lord shall preserve thee from all evil: he shall preserve thy soul. The Lord shall preserve thy going out and thy coming in from this time forth, and even for evermore" (Psalms 121:1-8).

29 April ~ "Safe Place"

I decided to take a break today and enjoy the beautiful, warm sun just like I had yesterday. As I sat in my XO chair in the sun, I felt safe. Though I felt safe inside the walls of the Compound, I knew that I had lots of fire power with those who were assigned to be the ultimate protectors and gunners. There's still the reality that this is a combat zone and we are at war with an enemy who hates us and what we stand for.

I closed my eyes and imagined I was lying on New Smyrna Beach in Florida. It was just that peaceful. But, the only **safe places** are under the wings of God's angels and in arms of Jesus. I also find comfort and safety in the scriptures.

"He that dwelleth in the secret place of the most High shall abide under the shadow of the Almighty. I will say of the LORD, He is my refuge and my fortress: my God; in him will I trust. Surely he shall deliver thee from the snare of the fowler, and from the noisome pestilence. He shall cover thee with his feathers, and under his wings shalt thou trust: his truth shall be thy shield and buckler. Thou shalt not be afraid for the terror by night; nor for the arrow that flieth by day; Nor for the pestilence that walketh in darkness; nor for the destruction that wasteth at noonday" (Psalms 91:1-6).

29 April ~ "Don't Call What I Made Dirty"

Tonight, while listening to the voice of God under my prayer shawl, He spoke to me boldly. **"Don't call what I made dirty."** My thought was, "I'm sorry Lord, I didn't call this place dirty, others did!" I thought about how most people warned me that Afghanistan was a dirty, filthy place. I had even read that many people died from air pollution rather than from the violence. I was told to leave my contacts at home because the air quality was so bad that it would cause continuous eye infections.

Maybe it's just still spring and not the hot summer in Afghanistan, but it has been beautiful! God sent record snow totals to purify the atmosphere (just for me), and we've had some rainy days to keep the dust under control.

God made Afghanistan just as He did every other place in this world. After He created it, He said it was good! I was talking to one of the cultural advisors, and he shared how God made this beautiful place, but man has destroyed that beauty because of their hate, violence, and desire for power.

Those words were so true. I see the beauty in Afghanistan that others don't. Flying across the skies of Afghanistan is one of the things I've enjoyed the most about my deployment. I love viewing the snow-capped mountains and valleys. We cannot call the things God created bad—Afghanistan is a piece of His handiwork.

I pray for peace, calmness, economic and agricultural prosperity for the people in Afghanistan.

"The earth is the Lord's, and the fulness thereof; the world, and they that dwell therein. For he hath founded it upon the seas, and established it upon the floods. Who shall ascend into the hill of the LORD? or who shall stand in his holy place? He that hath clean hands, and a pure heart; who hath not lifted up his soul unto vanity, nor sworn deceitfully" (Psalms 24:1-4).

30 April ~ "Are We Too Blessed?"

As we returned from a road trip to Bagram today, I mentioned to my Lead Mechanic that I refused to complain about not having something. I have witnessed so much desolation of the people in this country: children running beside the vehicles begging for food and money; women and babies in the middle of the street begging for food; and houses plastered into the hills and mountains with no running water or electricity.

The deprived children are forced to work and beg in the streets to provide for their families instead of attending school. Donkeys, sheep, goats, and dogs eat trash on the streets for food; they appear thin and malnourished. The devastation goes on and on.

"Oh God, forgive me for complaining!" I am so blessed and privileged that I don't always recognize it. My soul aches for a solution to help improve the living conditions of these people. I need to count my blessings and name them one by one! America is so blessed and yet she will fall if she trusts in riches. I am discouraged to see such paucity. Seeing this really makes me thankful for all the spiritual, physical, mental and financial blessings I have. But most of all, I am grateful for Jesus dying on the cross for my sins!

"The liberal soul shall be made fat: and he that watereth shall be watered also himself. He that withholdeth corn, the people shall curse him: but blessing shall be upon the head of him that selleth it. He that diligently seeketh good procureth favour: but he that seeketh mischief, it shall come unto him. He that trusteth in his riches shall fall: but the righteous shall flourish as a branch. He that troubleth his own house shall inherit the wind: and the fool shall be servant to the wise of heart. The fruit of the righteous is a tree of life; and he that winneth souls is wise. Behold, the righteous shall be recompensed in the earth: much more the wicked and the sinner" (Proverbs 11:25-31).

MAY 2012

1 May ~ "It's the President!"

While working late into the wee hours of the morning, I heard several low-flying helicopters overhead—nothing unusual. The person on CQ duty ran to the door to look outside, so I jumped up to see what was going on. They were U.S. helicopters carrying **President Obama** as they flew over our Compound. He was in Kabul to meet with Afghan President Karzai to sign an agreement regarding the drawdown of U.S. military forces.

Though we knew he didn't see us, we waved with honor as if he could. I went back to work and thought about how honored I felt in being in this country at this time, excited to be so close to the **President**! I also felt honored to be a member of a team of highly skilled professionals here to accomplish one of the nation's most sensitive missions.

I then felt honored to be a part of the Kingdom of God. Knowing that God allowed for **President Obama** to be in authority for this time period increased my belief that nothing happens without God's intervention and allowance. God is all powerful and allows certain things to happen as a part of His plan. I'm proud to be an American and honored to be a child of the King!

"Let every soul be subject unto the higher powers. For there is no power but of God: the powers that be are ordained of God. Whosoever therefore resisteth the power, resisteth the ordinance of God: and they that resist shall receive to themselves damnation" (Romans 13:1-2).

1 May ~ "I Need Thee"

During my prayer time in the early hours of the mornings, I confessed: "**I need thee** every hour Lord!"

Often when I'm under my prayer shawl, I feel like I can't breathe. I feel the confirmation weighing on me heavily—I need God! I can't breathe or move or live without Him. I ask Him to help me to more closely recognize my need for and dependence on Him!

"Lord, place me where You want me to be. Use me as an instrument of peace. When I return, place me in a new job where I can bring glory to You and my skills and light can shine. Thank You for being an on-time God!"

"Therefore is my spirit overwhelmed within me; my heart within me is desolate. I remember the days of old; I meditate on all thy works; I muse on the work of thy hands. I stretch forth my hands unto thee: my soul thirsteth after thee, as a thirsty land. Selah. Hear me speedily, O Lord: my spirit faileth: hide not thy face from me, lest I be like unto them that go down into the pit. Cause me to hear thy lovingkindness in the morning; for in thee do I trust: cause me to know the way wherein I should walk; for I lift up my soul unto thee" (Psalms 143:4-8).

2 May ~ "We Must Be Ready"

This morning I learned to always prep to the maximum the night before so that I can be ready for any emergency or situation during the night or early morning. I was awakened by a loud explosion at 0630 hours! I jumped straight up and ran to the bathroom to get myself ready to head to the bunker. I didn't have my clothes out, so I scrambled to get everything I needed, skipping part of my morning routine. I called CQ to find out what happened, but the person on duty didn't hear it. Then I heard the alarms go off!

There was an attack within the city close to our Compound. Later, we learned that about 70 people were killed, including children and school staff. The insurgents had blown up a building next to a school.

After all was calm, I sent a text to Frank and Chris to let them know all was well. Sometimes news coverage of incidents reached the U.S. before we ever found out about them. I felt it was important to keep them at ease with an "all is well" text.

We must be prepared and ready for the return of Christ. At any moment, on any day, He could return for His people. We can't be rushing around trying to get ready—**we must be ready**! You know—sleeping in your clothes—ready! This incident was so real to me. If it was my time to go, was I ready? YES! My heart is fixed and my mind is made up. To die in the Lord is live with Him forever. I'm reminded of words from a song written by my mother, Rita Sara Robinson Smith entitled, "Oh Let Me Die the Death of the Righteous."[3] She received the inspiration for this song from Numbers 23:10b.

Oh let me die the death of the righteous.
I want my last end to be like his.
I want to live a life so blameless,
That no soul may stumble over me.
And when my life here on earth will be finished,
I want the master to be pleased with me.
I want to live a life, a holy life, die a death, a righteous death.
That my last end will be like his.

"Behold, I shew you a mystery; We shall not all sleep, but we shall all be changed, In a moment, in the twinkling of an eye, at the last trump: for the trumpet shall sound, and the dead shall be raised incorruptible, and we shall be changed. Therefore, my beloved brethren, be ye stedfast, unmoveable, always abounding in the work of the Lord, forasmuch as ye know that your labour is not in vain in the Lord" (1 Corinthians 15: 51-52, 58).

---

[3] Rita Sara Robinson Smith. *Oh Let Me Die the Death of The Righteous.* November 16, 1967.

2 May ~ "Tune Out the Noise"

There are people who have prior military and combat experience or who have been previously deployed to Iraq that become accustomed to the explosions and are not alarmed by them. Some people just **tune out the noise** and continue on with their daily duties. There are others who are jumpy and tense whenever these incidents occur. Some people leave combat zones with emotional problems and suffer post-traumatic stress disorders.

Satan's attempts at distraction and destruction are difficult to tune out. But if we allow the peace of God to rule our hearts and minds, we can develop an immune system that will guard our hearts and minds against the real threats of the enemy. We have the weapons necessary to protect us: *"Finally, my brethren, be strong in the Lord, and in the power of his might. Put on the whole armour of God that ye may be able to stand against the wiles of the devil"* (Ephesians 6:10-11).

We will never be free from the enemy's attacks, but the noise can be tuned out to the point that we are not knocked down or rocked by it! We continue to let His Spirit keep us cool, calm and collected.

Tune out the noise of Satan and his devices so that we can continue to serve God and become busy working to build His Kingdom.

"And let the peace of God rule in your hearts, to the which also ye are called in one body; and be ye thankful. Let the word of Christ dwell in you richly in all wisdom; teaching and admonishing one another in psalms and hymns and spiritual songs, singing with grace in your hearts to the Lord" (Colossians 3:15-16).

3 May ~ "Time to Move"

I retreated to my room after a long day only to hear the sounds of dripping! Yep, my hot water heater had a crack in the seal around the opening and there was water all over the bathroom floor.

When we get to the place where the leaks in our lives are causing a flood, it is **time to make a move!** The problem needs to be addressed and so we can determine if the leak is repairable; if not, "it is **time to move.**"

Often this means moving away from the specific sin that is causing the leak. We must maintain the seals *"of our faith without wavering"* (Hebrews 10:23). We cannot allow Satan to poke any holes in our faith. We are sealed unto the day of redemption. We know that the day of the Lord is coming soon and we must not allow any leaks to cause damage to our spiritual houses.

"Let us hold fast the profession of our faith without wavering; (for he is faithful that promised;) And let us consider one another to provoke unto love and to good works: Not forsaking the assembling of ourselves together, as the manner of some is; but exhorting one another: and so much the more, as ye see the day approaching" (Hebrews 10:23-25).

4 May ~ "In it for the Money?"

Today I met with the new Executive Officer for one of our detachments. She seemed as if she got stuck with a job that she didn't really want, but felt the money was good, so she would do whatever to make it through her six months.

Prior to being deployed, lots of folks told me how deployment was great money and they would even go again just **for the money**. They had a great financial plan when they decided to deploy. In light of this, I began to think about my motives. I knew there would be monetary benefits, but that was not my primary goal for deploying. Wow, people would actually risk their lives just **for the money**! We must be careful not to let the *"love of money"* affect our decisions. Money is necessary to survive in this world, but *"the love of it is the root of all evil"* (1 Timothy 6:10).

I wondered how many people followed Jesus for the benefits (He fed 5,000 and healed the sick). How many people come to church for the benefits? And when some people don't get what they think they should at church, they'll stab you in the back and walk away.

We must be careful of those in our lives who only want to be with us to drain us of the benefits of the relationship.
No, I'm not in this **for the money**. I'm here to bring glory to God!

"For the love of money is the root of all evil: which while some coveted after, they have erred from the faith, and pierced themselves through with many sorrows" (1 Timothy 6:10).

5 May ~ "Peace in the Midst of the Storm"

It is really stormy in the office right now. Our Operations Support Chief has been on travel and will return tomorrow. Everyone is dreading her return. She causes so much havoc that people avoid her quite intentionally. I can't imagine how sad it would be to live in a situation where you're disliked by everyone. It must be miserable. She's been very vindictive, but I know that vengeance belongs to the Lord. She is one that does not belong here. Deployments are not for everyone.

You would not believe the heavy cloud that we endure some days. There have been some who stood up to her only to get reprimanded for being disrespectful. I did not allow my staff to be harassed by her. I would calmly and gently intervene and diffuse any argument or struggle with her. I would pray daily, asking God to help her to see her ways and change her heart.

At times God will still the storm; other times, He will give us the shelter and protection to survive the storm. Knowing who I am, I thank God for giving me **peace during this storm**. I will continue to promote a calm demeanor.

"Thou wilt keep him in perfect peace, whose mind is stayed on thee: because he trusteth in thee" (Isaiah 26:3).

6 May ~ "Life's Not Fair"

While praying, the words of a song ("My Savior I Shall See") we sang at my church were going through my mind:

> *My Savior I shall see will be enough for me.*
> *I'll praise Him for His sacrifice on cruel old Calvary.*
> *Someday I'll understand those pierced and wounded hands.*
> *And why he bore the cross for you and me.* (Source Unknown)

Why should I sacrifice the things that I want to have or do for someone else? Why do I have to take the abuse and say nothing when falsely accused or misused? Why do I have to give up so much while others continue to get, get and get more? **Life's not fair**!

Was it fair for Jesus to die on the cruel cross for the sins of the others, not committing any sin Himself? Was it fair that He got beat down by people He never knew or bothered? Was it fair that God had to give up His ONLY begotten Son to die as a sacrifice for you and me?

No! **It is not fair** and neither is life! I should be willing to go through some hard knocks in life because everything of every day is not going to go the way I want it. It's not about me and my wants. It's about what God has for me to do and say! I feel so undeserving of His love for me, especially when I don't always appreciate His sacrifice.

When we knowingly do wrong, we crucify Him all over again because we're saying, "I can't live above sin, I can't sacrifice a little of my wants and desires, Jesus. You can't save nor keep me." Think about what you're doing! If you know God, don't grieve Him with your unwillingness to sacrifice.

Why should I sacrifice? Why should I? Jesus did it and didn't have to—but thank God He did! I'm forever grateful for the sacrifice made just for me. This song came to mind: "Must Jesus Bear the Cross Alone?"[4]

Must Jesus bear the cross alone,
And all the world go free?
No, there's a cross for everyone,
And there's a cross for me.

"What shall we then say to these things? If God be for us, who can be against us? He that spared not his own Son, but delivered him up for us all, how shall he not with him also freely give us all things?" (Romans 8:31-32).

---

[4] George N. Allen, Thomas Shepherd. *Must Jesus Bear the Cross Alone?* © Words: Public Domain.

7 May ~ "Frustration"

As I was praying, I was feeling frustrated and overwhelmed. My mechanics were frustrated with the vehicles being down while they had neither parts nor tools to fix them.

Then the light bulb came on. I decided that instead of being frustrated, I would empower them to good works. We suffered difficulties in getting supplies through our logistical channels in headquarters. It would take months to receive simple items like toilet paper. The auto parts they ordered were held up for months. **Frustration** was an understatement!

I made an executive decision to let them order parts from local vendors to get them working. We ordered and got the majority of the parts the next day. I'm sure we paid more, but we're in a combat zone and need to keep the up-armored vehicles functional to support the operations. I love my job! I enjoy seeing people productive and empowered.

"My brethren, count it all joy when ye fall into divers temptations; Knowing this, that the trying of your faith worketh patience. But let patience have her perfect work, that ye may be perfect and entire, wanting nothing" (James 1:2-4).

8 May ~ "The Halfway Mark"

The excitement is surely there—God has blessed me to make it three months away from home, family and friends. He has blessed my health and spirit! I have attempted to remain positive and encourage others during this phase of the deployment. I've accomplished both spiritual and professional goals thus far.

As we look at life, **the halfway mark** could be on Earth one side and the other in heaven. I'm almost there—at 53, I'm closer to heaven than ever before. I know I can make it!

"I press toward the mark for the prize of the high calling of God in Christ Jesus" (Philippians 3:14).

9 May ~ "There's Good in Afghanistan"

Happy Birthday to my dear husband Frank! He called early to ask me what his surprise was going to be. The girls and grandkids showed up at the door for his birthday! The girls are so good to their father.

My day was uneventful, but I learned that there is at least one **good thing here in Afghanistan**—Pizza Hut! I get pizza almost every time I visit our other site in Kabul. It's freshly made to order. WOW, comfort food that reminds me of home. As Frank is being celebrated today with a beautiful dinner at Sullivan's, I thought about God granting me the desires of my heart with the American food that I am privileged to eat—Meat Lover's Pizza!

"Delight thyself also in the LORD: and he shall give thee the desires of thine heart" (Psalms 37:4).

10 May ~ "Change Your Light Bulb"

I asked our electrician to check the lighting in my room. There is dull lighting everywhere; the bathroom was the only bright room. He took the dull globes off and changed the light bulbs to the new swirling ones. Amazing! When I went into the room and flicked the lights on, I could see the computer so much better! The light will also help for writing.

Why not check your spiritual light bulb to see if you can shine brighter for Jesus Christ? In our spiritual lives, we must let our walk, our talk, and our actions be the light for others to see the Christ in us. If our lights are dim (our conversations are not uplifting or inappropriate), we could cause others to continue to walk and live in darkness.

What a difference it makes when one light bulb is changed to a new, brighter light. A bright light gets attention—you want your light to draw others to Christ. After all, it is one of the main reasons we remain on Earth.

"Let your light so shine before men, that they may see your good works, and glorify your Father which is in heaven" (Matthew 5:16).

10 May ~ "Deployment: The College Campus"

Since I attended college later in life, I didn't have the opportunity to stay in a dorm on campus. But this deployment gives me the same experience of being away from home, family, and friends, as well as learning new things and meeting new people. This Compound is like a small **college campus**. I go to class every day; I eat three times a day in the dining room; and we have activities together.

God is so merciful to me to allow me to experience "dorm life" in South Asia. I miss Frank, the kids, my grand-boys, family and friends. But, this adventure was needful for me at this time, and in this place.

I'm feeling grateful right now and need to express it. I still pinch myself to see if I'm awake and this is not a dream. There is NO way I could have done this without God's divine intervention and plan. Even physically, I see and feel improvements. "Thank You Lord!"

"For I know the thoughts that I think toward you, saith the LORD, thoughts of peace, and not of evil, to give you an expected end" (Jeremiah 29:11).

11 May ~ "But I Prayed, Lord"

As usual, I said a prayer prior to our exit from the Compound. The Lead Mechanic contractor was driving. One of our older vehicles, "Barney," was purple and beat up a bit, but normally reliable.

I mentioned to the Lead Mechanic that I always pray prior to leaving. About a half mile into the trip, the vehicle started making clunking noises; we were in trouble. I went into action mode based on my training, but never said, "Oh God what happened?—I

prayed!" Today I only prayed for safe travel to and from the destination. I didn't pray for the vehicle to not break down.

We pulled into a shopping center parking lot surrounded by Afghans trying to help. We were a little nervous, but we were thankful! The Lead Mechanic decided to drive the vehicle on the wrong side against the traffic to get us back quickly… it was a slow and bumpy ride, but we made it safely back to the Compound!

God did not say that we wouldn't have breakdowns or bumpy roads to travel. He said He would *"never leave us nor forsake us!"* He was so true to His promises today. He did just as I asked and gave us safe travel to and from our destination. We weren't harmed and we made it back safely.

But I prayed and He said, "Aw, look at my child in the middle of the street with car trouble. Let me send a few Afghans to help and have that mechanic turn around and get back to safety. You see, I was there all the time answering your prayer!"

Sister Cecelia Brooks from my home church says, "He may not come when you want Him, but He's always right on time. You can't hurry God, you just have to wait!"

"Because he hath set his love upon me, therefore will I deliver him: I will set him on high, because he hath known my name. He shall call upon me, and I will answer him: I will be with him in trouble; I will deliver him, and honour him" (Psalms 91:14-15).

12 May ~ "Self Sacrifice"

After a long night of Command Quarters (CQ) and only 45 minutes of sleep, the Communications Technician announced that there was a fire in the old workshop near the gate! I rushed out, radio in hand, to the front of the Compound. There was smoke billowing from the building! Everyone was grabbing fire extinguishers from every possible location. Three of my support team members were in there battling the flames with extinguishers and water.

Even though the local Afghan Fire Department and Police showed up, our heroes already had the fire under control. Our guards kept the firemen and policeman up front near the gate for security purposes, to avoid access to the remainder of the Compound. We were amazed at the record time it took the Fire

Department to arrive. Later, we discovered that our Afghan Guard Commander was friends with the Fire Chief.

Only God could have allowed this miracle to happen on this day. There were propane tanks and other HAZMATs in the workshop, yet there was no explosion! God, with His loving protection, put a shield around us. Those old tanks should have blown up; they were leaking gas when they brought them out of the burning building and sat them in an open area of the front of the Compound.

Our Afghan guards were right alongside our staff, fighting the fire, pulling items from the building and pulling the water hoses to the building. Per request of the Fire Chief, our Cultural Advisors asked the female Ops Support Chief and me to leave because our heads weren't covered. My thought was, "excuse me, this is our Compound, and we're fighting a fire here, what's the issue?" I took a deep prayer breath and became submissive and obedient and we moved back to provide radio assistance out of the sight of the Afghan firemen. It's a known cultural requirement that the women cover their heads in public. Even on our own territory, humility is a godly characteristic, which I had to display on this day.

This was such a show of heroic selfless acts; the Commander was quite impressed. I was amazed with what teamwork can do for a group of folks. It just shows that, in an emergency situation, people put aside all personal issues and join in to save lives and property. The major issue for us was protecting our location from exposure. I was so thankful for the **self-sacrifice** demonstrated and the protection of a loving God.

"Greater love hath no man than this, that a man lay down his life for his friends" (John 15:13).

12 May ~ "Fighting the Flames"

After the fire, we had an "after action review" round table. We reviewed what happened, gathered the facts from those close to the emergency, and discussed what we needed to do to ensure the safety of the Compound and property as we moved forward.

I thought about the times we see our family or friends on fire with the flames of the enemy, burning them in preparation for Hell, and we have no water or extinguisher there to help save them.

"Lord, let our selfless impulse come forth **to fight the flames** of the enemy for our children, family and friends." Some of our kids are too close to the propane tank and are about to explode, living the sinful life with no care in the world. "God, please put that shield around them and perform Your miracle to have someone to extinguish the flames just as You did for us on 12 May 2012! Give us the firepower to encourage and persuade them to accept your Son Jesus and turn instead of burn."

"Son of man, I have made thee a watchman unto the house of Israel: therefore hear the word at my mouth, and give them warning from me. When I say unto the wicked, Thou shalt surely die; and thou givest him not warning, nor speakest to warn the wicked from his wicked way, to save his life; the same wicked man shall die in his iniquity; but his blood will I require at thine hand. Yet if thou warn the wicked, and he turn not from his wickedness, nor from his wicked way, he shall die in his iniquity; but thou hast delivered thy soul" (Ezekiel 3: 17–19).

13 May ~ "My First Tear"

I was thanking God all last night for His divine protection from the fire yesterday. After wishing everyone a Happy Mother's Day, I began to conduct my morning briefing. I thanked the heroes for their selfless acts and everyone who worked hard to put out the fire. I mentioned the fact that the three propane tanks leaking gas didn't explode because God was protecting us from harm. The Fire Chief told the Guard Commander that if they had been in there a few minutes more, they would have exploded. But for God!

I was overcome with gratitude and told the staff that God had performed a miracle on this Compound and that I was grateful to be amongst a group of professionals on whom I could depend on in a crisis. This was **my first tear** shed, specifically in front of people. You could hear a pin drop in the room, as others also shed tears. As much as I tried to be stern and professional, I broke down because the love God resting upon me for people had its way. Our Commander followed up with his gratitude toward everyone who had a part in resolving the emergency.

At our next Hail and Farewell, I received a new call sign: "Mother Hen." The senior officer felt it appropriate as I had demonstrated a love and special care for the staff just like a mother!

"O give thanks unto the LORD; call upon his name: make known his deeds among the people" (Psalms 105:1).

13 May ~ "The Double Rainbow"

It was a cloudy, sunny and rainy day! I went to our other site with one of my Security Team members to check on the staff there. The weather was looking bad; it was windy, clouds and dust were everywhere. We arrived at the building when the rain poured in big loud drops.

Once we finished our business there, we walked outside to see the sun shining very brightly. Then we saw not just one, but two rainbows. What a beautiful sight—a **double rainbow**. I began to share the purpose of the rainbow and the story of Noah with my Security Team member. He shared that he grew up as a churchgoer in his teen years, but left due to hypocrisy. He said he still has his faith in God, but he is not as faithful as he was in his youth. I shared with him that as adults, it is important to share our stories with other people who will be moved to come to Christ.

Thank God for the double rainbow that can give us a reminder of the importance of sharing our faith with others. I prayed that God would move on his heart to become a faithful disciple.

"And I will establish my covenant with you; neither shall all flesh be cut off any more by the waters of a flood; neither shall there anymore be a flood to destroy the earth. And God said, This is the token of the covenant which I make between me and you and every living creature that is with you, for perpetual generations: I do set my bow in the cloud, and it shall be for a token of a covenant between me and the earth. And it shall come to pass, when I bring a cloud over the earth, that the bow shall be seen in the cloud: And I will remember my covenant, which is between me and you and every living creature of all flesh; and the waters shall no more become a flood to destroy all flesh. And the bow shall be in the cloud; and I will look upon it, that I may remember the everlasting covenant between God and every living creature of all flesh that is upon the earth. And God said unto Noah, This is the token of the covenant, which I have established between me and all flesh that is upon the earth" (Genesis 9:11-17).

14 May ~ "The Road Less Traveled"

I went to Bagram today in a convoy of two vehicles. I rode with one of our Cultural Advisors on the return back to the Compound. The ride was about 45 minutes through dangerous areas known to be enemy-insurgent heavy. This Cultural Advisor decided to take a different, "safer" route.

This road was so bumpy that we had to drive very slowly. It was the "**road less traveled**" by those who traveled to and from Bagram. The other driver complained over the radio and asked why we were taking a route which was scenic, slow, bumpy and narrow. The purpose was so that we all could learn another route in case there was an insurgency incident or checkpoint on the normal route.

I thought about our walk with Christ. Many want the wide and broad way so they can go fast without dips and holes to slow them down. They don't want the way of Jesus Christ because it cramps their style. We have to have a close walk with God and keep His commandments. People today want a quick, feel-good message so they can go home to do nothing that honors God.

The straight and narrow way leads to life eternal. This way may be bumpy sometimes with trials and tribulations, but you'll eventually arrive safely at your eternal destination.

"Because strait is the gate, and narrow is the way, which leadeth unto life, and few there be that find it" (Matthew 7:14).

15 May ~ "Basic Necessities"

We had a busy morning due to the delivery of our food and water. I was discouraged when some folks didn't come to help, and instead went on their way. I thought: "here are our **basic necessities** and people don't even come to help with the delivery and storage of the very items that they'll devour later in the day."

Getting our **basic necessities**—food and water—are essential for our survival out here. We attempt to get sufficient amounts in case we're locked down for an unspecified amount of time. If we don't get these basics, it could be detrimental to our survival.

So as it is with God. He gives us our basic necessities through His word. *"And Jesus being full of the Holy Ghost returned from Jordan,*

95

and was led by the Spirit into the wilderness, Being forty days tempted of the devil. And in those days he did eat nothing: and when they were ended, he afterward hungered. And the devil said unto him, If thou be the Son of God, command this stone that it be made bread. And Jesus answered him, saying, It is written, That man shall not live by bread alone, but by every word of God" (Luke 4: 1-4).

Food is good and essential, but unless you are eating the Word of God, you'll starve and die spiritually. Our **basic necessities** from God's Word are to believe and accept Him so you'll have everlasting life. Don't be fooled by Satan's temptations to ingest other things; eat the Word!

"But he answered and said, It is written, Man shall not live by bread alone, but by every word that proceedeth out of the mouth of God" (Matthew 4:4).

16 May ~ "Uneventful, But a Good Day"

Today began sunny; then the rainstorm brought violent hail. I thanked God for the fresh rain, which cleaned the air and kept down the dust.

Even though it was an **uneventful day**, no two days are the same. I had quite a bit listed on the To Do List, specifically to get my operational funds account balanced. That was one significant item I was able to cross off the list, which made this a very **good day**.

I rejoiced as I thought about how I may not have accomplished everything that I had on my list, but it was a mighty **good day**! I'm just thankful to God for the little things in life.

"This is the day which the LORD hath made; we will rejoice and be glad in it" (Psalms 118:24).

17 May ~ "Ground Guide"

Upon arrival at one of the other sites, I had to be a **ground guide** while my driver drove to our destination. A **ground guide** is the person who walks on foot in front of a vehicle to guide it to its destination slowly. The ground guide keeps the vehicle moving at a safe speed to help avoid any incidents on roads throughout the

Compound. There are so many people and vehicles sharing the roadways that the military has instituted this safety measure to ensure there are no accidents on the Compound. Reducing speed is the major purpose of a **ground guide**.

The words of the song, "He Goes Before Me" that was sung in my church came to my mind:

> *He goes before me and watches over me,*
> *While on my journey, I'll press along.*
> *He'll never forsake me, my Jesus will take me.*
> *While on my journey, I'll press along.* (Source Unknown)

While on this Earth, Jesus will be our "**ground guide**" from day to day, but only if we want to be led. We can't just run ahead of Him because things are not going fast enough for us. We must obey His "legal speed limits". Let Jesus be your **"Ground Guide."**

"For thou art my rock and my fortress; therefore for thy name's sake lead me, and guide me." (Psalms 31:3).

18 May ~ "Today I Prayed for You'

I dedicate this teachable moment to my spiritual daughter, Alisha.
Alisha just celebrated her 30th birthday a few weeks ago; what a milestone in her life—to reach 30!

I talked to her today about her professional goals, reviewed her resume with her, and provided professional advice and guidance for federal government and private sector job opportunities.

Today I prayed for her as she shared some new events in her life. I prayed that God would guide her in her decision making. I prayed that the decisions she made were in His plan. My prayer for Alisha: "God, You have a plan for her. You have taken her through things in life that will forever affect her and she needs your loving touch to help her settle in Your Word. Help her to be one with You. AMEN!"

"And we know that all things work together for good to them that love God, to them who are the called according to his purpose" (Romans 8:28).

19 May ~ "Happy Anniversary Frank"

This teachable moment is dedicated to my dear husband,
Francis Glenn Smith, Sr.!

Even though we are far, far apart, we still have such a bond that we think of each other at the same time.

Here are my thoughts: "Well, we made it to 33 years of marriage; though it was difficult as youngsters, we were learning to live with one another. God continues to have His hands on this union. What God joined together, no man could put a wedge between. We are such a great team!

We enjoy being together and entertaining family and friends. We pretty much agreed on most issues as we raised our children. We look at them and marvel at how God has blessed them. Now we are in-laws and grandparents. WOW! God has truly smiled on us to enjoy this, another milestone.

Thank You God, for putting us together and keeping us together! I Love You Francis!"

"Wherefore they are no more twain, but one flesh. What therefore God hath joined together, let not man put asunder" (Matthew 19:6).

19 May ~ "The Eraser"

As I prepped my first journal book for the final pages, I had to **erase** some notes of a list of items my daughter, Kamille, wanted to buy and send to me. I **erased** them, noticing that I didn't get all the pencil marks off the page.

When we try to clean up our own lives, we sometimes leave blemishes and stains behind. I thought about this scripture: *"Come now, and let us reason together, saith the LORD: though your sins be as scarlet, they shall be as white as snow; though they be red like crimson, they shall be as wool"* (Isaiah 1:18).

Only the God we serve can take the dirt and messed-up life that we have lived and **erase** the stains, mess and dirt. When He **erases** and puts our sins far away, they are never to return. He said He wouldn't remember them, either. He can wipe the slate clean after we confess and repent—giving us an opportunity to start afresh and move forward in a new life.

What God has **erased**, don't try to bring it back! Don't return to the mud and wallow in it after being cleaned. Thank God for being the ultimate **Eraser**!

"If we confess our sins, he is faithful and just to forgive us our sins, and to cleanse us from all unrighteousness" (1 John 1:9).

20 May ~ "To Be Alone with You"

Technically, it is Sunday… it is 0230 hours. My Tallit Prayer Message as I was listening to God was, "What does it mean **to be Alone with God?**"

"Lord, I'm here to get closer to You. I feel it is important to develop a closer relationship with You, to know You better, deeper, richer, and more intimately. For me, the only way is to get away and **be alone with You!**

Being alone with You makes me feel like I have Your total attention; I have You all to myself. I can talk to You with no interruptions. I feel Your loving presence all around me, from my room to the top of the roof where I can grasp Your handiwork.

When I see the snow-capped mountains or a double rainbow, I am in awe of Your glory and majesty. God, there is NONE like You. **Being alone with You** makes me feel humbled, yet empowered with boldness. God, Your awesome presence in this place is unspeakable. Being in Your presence is so unexplainable. My earthly wisdom cannot decipher it. **Being alone with You** is like being in another place; it is celestial, like no other place I've been before. I'm just an ordinary person, yet I feel so special in Your presence. Special, but unworthy of Your grace and mercy. I don't deserve any of it, but I'm so grateful that You bestowed these gifts upon me.

I'm in a strange land with strange people, people who do not know You like I know You. Yet, I am no better than they are; some long for that relationship with You. Grant it, dear Lord, grant them the desires of their hearts to know and worship the one and only true God - the God of Israel.

The only safe place is in Your presence. I love **being alone with You**, talking and listening to You! You alone are worthy of all praise. I love the free-flowing thoughts You have given me to write. You are a jealous God and will have no other gods before

You. You want Your people to love, reverence, and submit to Your will for their lives.

Help us Lord…Help ME to be what You want me to be; go where You want me to go; say what You want me to say, and do what You want me to do. God, You are awesome and I can't breathe, live, or do anything without You in my life. I need Thee every hour, minute, and second. I'm in a place where I don't want to leave…that's in Your presence—**Alone with You!**"

"And Jacob awaked out of his sleep, and he said, Surely the Lord is in this place; and I knew it not. And he was afraid, and said, How dreadful is this place! this is none other but the house of God, and this is the gate of heaven" (Genesis 28:16-17).

"Oh how great is thy goodness, which thou hast laid up for them that fear thee; which thou hast wrought for them that trust in thee before the sons of men! Thou shalt hide them in the secret of thy presence from the pride of man: thou shalt keep them secretly in a pavilion from the strife of tongues" (Psalms 31:19-20).

"Surely the righteous shall give thanks unto thy name: the upright shall dwell in thy presence" (Psalms 140:13).

"The name of the Lord is a strong tower: the righteous runneth into it, and is safe" (Proverbs 18:10).

21 May ~ "The Cracked Foundation"

While talking to my Staff Director at the home office today, I mentioned that we had another earthquake!

Actually, the earthquake was in Iran, but we got our share of the rumble and damage. We had cracks on the outside of some buildings and plaster falling from others. Otherwise, we were okay. Our Facilities Manager had someone come and check the buildings and fix the large cracks.

This was a powerful lesson when I thought about being in a building with **cracks and an unstable foundation**! Any additional shifting of the foundation, and we could see a tumbling building.

We may try to build on another's foundation, but spiritually we can only stand on one—Jesus Christ, who is our rock and salvation! On His foundation, there are no cracks or falling plaster. There is no wavering or shifting. Jesus is the sure foundation.

Often, people live and attempt to build on a foundation not knowing whether it is solid. Take heed of where you put your trust, hopes, and dreams. Be certain it is grounded on a sure foundation and according to God's plan.

"According to the grace of God which is given unto me, as a wise masterbuilder, I have laid the foundation, and another buildeth thereon. But let every man take heed how he buildeth thereupon. For other foundation can no man lay than that is laid, which is Jesus Christ. Now if any man build upon this foundation gold, silver, precious stones, wood, hay, stubble; Every man's work shall be made manifest: for the day shall declare it, because it shall be revealed by fire; and the fire shall try every man's work of what sort it is" (1 Corinthians 3:10-13).

22 May ~ "Shut Up and Listen"

I was finding it quite hard tonight to **shut up and listen**. Prayer is a two-way communication. Yet so often I have so many people on my heart and so many issues in my life that I try to get them all out in one prayer session!

I need to try focusing on a few each night and reserve time for listening. God does have something to say and I don't want to miss it!

I'm still seeking to master the gift of listening.

"Be still, and know that I am God: I will be exalted among the heathen, I will be exalted in the earth" (Psalms 46:10).

"Teach me, and I will hold my tongue: and cause me to understand wherein I have erred" (Job 6:24).

23 May ~ "The Church and the Family"

During our Bible Study session tonight, someone referred to the similarities of the **church** structure and the **family**.

Our **church** has always been comprised of families and functioned as a **family**. When one hurts, the others hurt. When one rejoices, we all rejoice. Our Founder and leader was like a father figure. The First Lady of the church normally functions in a motherly role.

When family members get married, they add others to the family; spouses and children. Thus, the family grows.

In the **church**, we reach out and encourage others to come and join the **family** of God. The church grows and we all live happily ever after...not literally. Just as we have issues in the **family**, we have issues with one another in the **church**.

Instead of a social club, the **church** should function more like a **family** that prays together and stays together. A marriage and family which follows God's instructions will be lasting, productive, and happy.

"So ought men to love their wives as their own bodies. He that loveth his wife loveth himself. For no man ever yet hated his own flesh; but nourisheth and cherisheth it, even as the Lord the church: For we are members of his body, of his flesh, and of his bones. For this cause shall a man leave his father and mother, and shall be joined unto his wife, and they two shall be one flesh. This is a great mystery: but I speak concerning Christ and the church" (Ephesians 5:28-32).

24 May ~ "When I Am Wrong"

Today I had a verbal confrontation with the thorn in my side—the Type A soul. Later, I did apologize to her to let her know that I was wrong.

No one wants to think they can actually be wrong about something, especially when it is about work, opinions, or relationships. Accepting and acknowledging you're wrong is difficult, but necessary in our Christian walk.

God requires us to confess the sin, be sorry, and don't repeat it! You would think that it would be easy not to repeat the sin, but Satan knows our weaknesses and he'll continue to throw that same issue at us time after time to throw us off balance and make us fall again. We must learn from our sins and vow not to repeat them. Only through perseverance and the Holy Ghost can we combat and conquer the enemy and strive for perfection in that matter.

It is hard when you're dealing with people who constantly get under your skin. We have to recognize that it's not the person, but

Satan using the person to get at us—don't entertain him. **When we are wrong**, we must make it right! Forgiveness and repentance are all we need to overcome.

"Confess your faults one to another, and pray one for another, that ye may be healed. The effectual fervent prayer of a righteous man availeth much" (James 5:16).

"Be ye angry, and sin not: let not the sun go down upon your wrath: Neither give place to the devil" (Ephesians 4:26-27).

25 May ~ "M. R. E."

We experienced an issue with getting approval for our Class I food service. We were running out of food; we had about three days of supply remaining to feed 45-50 people. Believe me, God had a plan.

Then I thought about **MREs** (meals ready to eat) and how military members have used them for years to survive on the battlefield and during desolate conditions. Surviving on peanut butter and jelly isn't the ideal meal, but I've heard these military **MREs** are supposed to be good. They even have choices now. Times have changed.

We should keep the Word in our hearts so we can be ready to consume it when spiritually hungry and respond to anyone who asks the reason why we serve Him. When you find your spirit starving or suffering from malnutrition, check the aisle labeled: Jesus! He'll supply your every need.

Now, that was some good eating!

"Thy words were found, and I did eat them; and thy word was unto me the joy and rejoicing of mine heart: for I am called by thy name, O LORD God of hosts" (Jeremiah 15:16).

25 May ~ "Highlight the Significant"

When I study or review documents, I normally **highlight** the passages or material I read which I want to remember or come back to later as a reference. This information is what I need to commit it to memory or review again.

We should **highlight** the words that the Holy Spirit reveals to us in order for the words to be brought back to our memory when needed; these are words of comfort or guidance to calm our fears or defeat the enemy.

"Thy word have I hid in mine heart, that I might not sin against thee. Open thou mine eyes, that I may behold wondrous things out of thy law" (Psalms 119:11, 18).

25 May ~ "The T-Walls"

While I was at the construction site on our other Compound, I was watching the workers erect huge **T-Walls** to enclose a parking area. They had gigantic cranes with heavy chains to lift the concrete walls from a huge forklift. The men worked as a team to get the walls placed strategically next to each other to create a secure wall.

T-Walls are very large (12-15 feet high, 4 feet wide and 2 feet thick) concrete barriers placed to protect personnel from direct or indirect small arms fire, mortars, rockets, and shrapnel. **T-Walls** surround almost every building or tent; they line the streets in the Green Zone and every check point in Afghanistan.

The Word of God serves as our **T-Wall**—to protect us from the enemy of our souls.

"Every word of God is pure: he is a shield unto them that put their trust in him" (Proverbs 30:5).

26 May ~ "A Proud Father"

I was sharing with my Commander that I was a grandmother. He shared the success of his son in his job pursuits. We both acknowledged how blessed and proud we were of our children.

As we are pleased with our children when they make great or small accomplishments, we feel so proud of them. Such a sense of gratitude and success! It is a joy to see your children succeed and prosper.

The same is true of God! He is overflowing with pleasure when we, as His children, are successful. He rejoices when we accomplish the commission to win souls for Him. When we stand strong against wrong, He's smiling. When we use our gifts and talents to His glory and honor, He's well pleased.

My prayer is that my heavenly **Father is as proud** of me as my earthly father. I want to bring glory to His name and not bring dishonor nor re-crucify His Son Jesus on the cross! I want Him to say, *"Well done good and faithful servant."*

When we do the will of the Lord, He is well pleased. Just think: He's a **Proud Father**!

"Lord, make me an instrument to be used by You and not by man—to bring souls to Christ and glorify Your name. This is your child's prayer—AMEN!"

"His lord said unto him, Well done, thou good and faithful servant: thou hast been faithful over a few things, I will make thee ruler over many things: enter thou into the joy of thy lord" (Matthew 25:21).

27 May ~ "You Must Be Certified"

In the recent weeks, we have been dealing with the denial to receive Class I food service. This was due to the expiration of our previous paperwork and the fact that we do not have a certified cook or kitchen. We have Afghan cooks who are not "kitchen certified" in accordance with Army regulations.

We've investigated obtaining MREs, joking about crackers and water, but no one wants to have this issue of no food for 45-50 people. The Commander has lost sleep over this issue. I sleep fine because I know the Father will never leave me nor forsake me. He will provide manna! This Compound will have food because one of His children resides here.

In order to get the Class I status with God, **you must be certified**; everyone can obtain Class I status with God, washed by the blood of Jesus and cleansed from all sin, this certification is a process—you can't cheat or get it overnight. Sometimes you must go by way of experiencing trial by fire and demonstrate your worthiness to meet the Master's will. Living holy and righteous will get you certified!

"That if thou shalt confess with thy mouth the Lord Jesus, and shalt believe in thine heart that God hath raised him from the dead, thou shalt be saved" (Romans 10:9).

28 May ~ "Don't Remember Me Next Year"

During our morning briefing, the Commander mentioned that Memorial Day is to remember the fallen soldiers who died in support of our country's freedom. He said, **"I don't want to remember any of you next year."** His point was for us to be safe and continue to be vigilant to ensure a safe return home.

War is inevitable so long as we live on this Earth. With war, there are always casualties on either side. As we honor our fallen soldiers, I'm reminded of my monthly church publication, *The Happy News*. The May monthly edition each year is filled with pictures of church members; not fallen, but elevated to the next level toward heaven to forever be with our loving God and Son Jesus Christ.

What a gathering that will be—all of God's children together at our new home to forever worship and praise God for being God of all the universe!

I remember with admiration, reverence and respect, the saints who have gone on before us, for their lives meant so much to those of us they left behind. As godly examples and encouragers in the faith, their death is priceless.

As good soldiers, the saints have been faithful until death and will receive the crown of life. (Revelations 2:10.)

"For as in Adam all die, even so in Christ shall all be made alive" (1 Corinthians 15:22).

28 May ~ "No One is a Lost Cause"

During my Tallit prayer, God dropped this in my spirit. We've all heard the phrase, **"lost cause,"** in other words, something or someone that is hopeless. Some people live such riotous lives or are so mean-spirited, that we see no hope in repentance or recovery for them. But God, thankfully, doesn't see these souls like we do. *"His thoughts are not our thoughts; His ways are not our ways."*

Even on her last day, Type A was mad at me for something! I shook my head and felt sorry for her in her continued dislike and resentment towards me. I took out a nice card I had to give to her, but then changed my mind as I felt she would make a scene in front of everyone. So I just gave her a smile and wave to bid her farewell. She returned the gesture, and my heart was at peace!

But, her team members were smirking and whispering that the vehicle needed to hurry up and leave. She had such a negative impact on at least 95% of the Compound residents. It was sad that one person had such a bad influence which affected everyone!

I continue to pray for her, because I realize that she was a soul that needed hope and salvation! With God, nothing is impossible, and as long as there is breath in the body, there are no **lost causes**! Everyone will have an opportunity to accept Jesus!

"I exhort therefore, that, first of all, supplications, prayers, intercessions, and giving of thanks, be made for all men; For kings, and for all that are in authority; that we may lead a quiet and peaceable life in all godliness and honesty. For this is good and acceptable in the sight of God our Saviour; Who will have all men to be saved, and to come unto the knowledge of the truth. For there is one God, and one mediator between God and men, the man Christ Jesus; Who gave himself a ransom for all, to be testified in due time" (1 Timothy 2:1-6).

29 May ~ "It's All in Who You Know"

I was afforded the opportunity to accompany my Commander to a meeting with some top leaders in the Joint Staff. Through this, I learned the importance of relationships. He made contact with another Marine Colonel who was in a position to help our Unit with some issues. I was able to interject and raise additional issues where we needed assistance. The Colonel put us in contact with the right people to get a site visit of the location where we wanted to place a temporary trailer as a meeting space. As you build relationships through acquaintances, people are willing to help with the development of your project.

As we build our relationships in the Body of Christ, and when we have a need, we can count on those acquaintances to come to our aide. The same concept is true as we build our relationship with Jesus Christ. He introduces us to the big boss—God himself! **It's all in who you know!**

"He that walketh with wise men shall be wise: but a companion of fools shall be destroyed" (Proverbs 13:20).

30 May ~ "The Way Ahead"

Today I responded to the Platform HQ Chief regarding issues that were not being resolved. I also provided solutions and a **way ahead** for consideration. In today's business, if you don't have a solution to a problem, you don't have a voice. My purpose is to improve processes and make life easier for the staff I serve. Most issues were long-term and never addressed appropriately. Previous folk just let it go, but I refused!

In order to move ahead and progress, you must know and understand where you've been and the goal you wish to achieve. I refused to give up on a failed process that needed resolution. I was able to get HQ leadership's buy-in on an improvement to the logistical process, which improved visibility and reduced the time which it took to process supply requirements.

Some new Christians look back only to help with their forward plans for a closer walk with God. Once you're on the road forward, you'll have a clearer view of **"the way ahead!"**

"Thou wilt shew me the path of life: in thy presence is fulness of joy; at thy right hand there are pleasures for evermore" (Psalms 16:11).

"Teach me thy way, O LORD, and lead me in a plain path, because of mine enemies" (Psalms 27:11).

31 May ~ "Your Plan, Not Mine"

As I was praying today, God put Lisa on my mind. Lisa is a friend and fellow member of our church. She was diagnosed with an inoperable tumor. I received a text from my husband, Frank that they were taking her off life support and transferring her back to hospice. This news greatly saddened me. Lisa was a great inspiration to her family, and all the children in the Gospel

Spreading Church of God loved her! To see her go this way was disconcerting.

We all kept asking God to heal her from the cancerous tumor. In our eyes, we saw a person who was so giving and whose gifts were always being used in God's service. It was hard to accept the fact that God was saying, "Come and be with Me, Lisa."

I can only surmise that He had a plan and I must trust Him, though it wasn't my heart's desire. "For it is **Your plan God, not mine** or anyone else's. God, please bless the family—give them strength and comfort as only You can."

"There are many devices in a man's heart; nevertheless the counsel of the Lord, that shall stand" (Proverbs 19:21).

JUNE 2012

1 June ~ "Lord, Make Me Better"

During my Tallit prayer time, the Lord put in my spirit a desire to be **better**. I want to forever grow in grace and increase in knowledge and understanding. Growing in grace and developing spiritually are imperative to overall improvement or betterment. I want God to mold me, like the potter forms the clay when perfecting his prized piece.

There's always room for improvement and I'm all for it. This deployment has allowed me to grow and become **better** at what God has planned for me to accomplish. "Lord, I always want to be in a position and have the mindset for You to **make me better!**"

"The word which came to Jeremiah from the LORD, saying: "Arise and go down to the potter's house, and there I will cause you to hear my words." Then I went down to the potter's house, and, behold, he wrought a work on the wheels. And the vessel that he made of clay was marred in the hand of the potter: so he made it again another vessel, as seemed good to the potter to make it" (Jeremiah 18:1-4).

2 June ~ "Words of Encouragement from Home"

I was so encouraged today when I got the mail! It is always like Christmas around here when you get mail. Today I learned a lesson about the covering protection of God and the value of those folks at home. You know that everyone is praying for you and thinking about you while you're away, but when you actually get something from home that touches your heart deeply; it's a divine gift from God.

I received a package from Sister Ruth G. Robinson with a letter and cards signed by the Church of God members in Newport News and Hampton, VA. I was so humbled at the reading of each name and word of encouragement sent "special delivery" for me.

Today I received four cards from Sister Doris "California" Coates. She has labeled each card for each month that I am deployed! So thoughtful…each card has a special place in my heart.

So I dedicate this teachable moment to all who sent words of encouragement. Your love demonstrated and ministry in serving my needs has strengthened me to grow closer to God.

"For God is not unrighteous to forget your work and labour of love, which ye have shewed toward his name, in that ye have ministered to the saints, and do minister (Hebrews 6:10).

2 June ~ "No Badging in Heaven"

As I sat in a lounge chair, I closed my eyes for a moment and daydreamed that I was on New Smyrna Beach, Florida. I could almost feel it in the air—warm and sunny with a light breeze…WAKE UP girl, you're in Afghanistan!

I had to get up really early today so that I could get to the Compound where we were erecting a new facility. We'd hired an Afghan company to do the work and were responsible for overseeing their work and escorting them while they were on the Compound.

Getting these workers on site was a two-hour process today. Three had badges, while the other four did not. They stood in line until they were checked off the handwritten list. I then examined how the workers methodically chopped the tall grass with a little sickle, which was manual labor like I've never witnessed before.

The **badging process** caused me to reinforce this well-known lesson: if you don't have the Holy Spirit, you can't be "a write-in." Not everyone will make it to heaven, but, we all will make it to the great judgment. We'll stand before the Great Judge and answer for all the things we've done, both good and evil. There will be no line, no waiting for a badge to get in. We all want to hear God say, *"Well done thy good and faithful servant."*

"His lord said unto him, Well done, good and faithful servant; thou hast been faithful over a few things, I will make thee ruler over many things: enter thou into the joy of thy lord" (Matthew 25:23).

3 June ~ "No Chlorine?"

As I was carrying out my daily duties, I entered the water shed to add chlorine and water to the holding tank. Much to my surprise, there was **no chlorine** in the bucket. We were out of a chemical essential to keeping us all healthy.

I thought about how the chlorine was similar to the Holy Spirit whom we need so we can daily perform in a godly manner. Just as the water needs the chlorine, we need the cleansing of the Holy Spirit to bring good to the world. Without it, we have no effect on the body of unbelievers. The Holy Spirit is the potent purification power that rids our hearts and minds of harmful ungodly thoughts and desires.

We need to stock up quickly!

"But ye shall receive power, after that the Holy Ghost is come upon you: and ye shall be witnesses unto me both in Jerusalem, and in all Judaea, and in Samaria, and unto the uttermost part of the earth" (Acts 1:8).

3 June ~ "Anointing, Fall On Me"

During my Tallit prayer time, I was worshiping God for the opportunity to partake in the holy sacrament of communion. This is the first Sunday of the month, and I brought along six communion sets so I could be a part of my church's communion service from afar.

I worshiped God for the ultimate sacrifice made by His Son to shed His blood and offer up His body just for me. I felt **God's anointing** over me during this prayer time. Being in His presence is an awesome, adulating experience. It is an experience that you never want to end. What a great privilege it will be to partake of the communion elements with Jesus in the Kingdom of God.

"And as they did eat, Jesus took bread, and blessed, and brake it, and gave to them, and said, Take, eat: this is my body. And he took the cup, and when he had given thanks, he gave it to them: and they all drank of it. And he said unto them, This is my blood of the new testament, which is shed for many. Verily I say unto you, I will drink no more of the fruit of the vine, until that day that I drink it new in the kingdom of God" (Mark 14:22-25).

4 June ~ "Released for Transition"

Lord, what a hard pill to swallow today. Frank sent me a text to let me know that our friend and fellow church member, Lisa, transitioned today from this life here on Earth to be with the Lord. I thought about how God **released her for this transition**.

There are transitions we must make in life that we never reach because we failed to let go or release. Webster's Dictionary has termed the word *transition* as "a passage from one state, stage, subject, or place to another."[5] When we hold onto things that are not productive, they will hinder our ability to transition to the next level. I often hear federal workers complain about being held back by "the man," when in actuality, they are the person responsible for their stagnant condition.

God has given us His word to help us grow in wisdom and knowledge. As we open our hearts for more of God, we can be freed from the obligation of sin, and therefore **transition** on to higher heavenly grounds. Receiving God's Spirit now will ensure a smooth **transition** when it is our time to be **released**.

"Precious in the sight of the Lord is the death of his saints." (Psalms 116:15)

"For the Lord himself shall descend from heaven with a shout, with the voice of the archangel, and with the trump of God: and the dead in Christ shall rise first: Then we which are alive and remain shall be caught up together with

---

[5] (http://www.merriam-webster.com/dictionary/transition; accessed February 27, 2013).

them in the clouds, to meet the Lord in the air: and so shall we ever be with the Lord" (1 Thessalonians 4:16-17).

5 June ~ "Let the Words of My Mouth"

I learned today that the new Senior Logistician will be assigned to our Compound instead of Bagram as requested and needed. I prayed that God would guard my tongue that I would not bring a reproach to His name.

You see, this employee was not well received here by those who are long-term employees. When he was here before, he caused a lot of friction and was downright mean to the staff. He treated the contractors like second-class citizens and cursed them continuously. In fact, they pleaded with me to have him sent elsewhere because they felt they could not work with his cantankerous demeanor. He was assigned to the Bagram Compound for the first four weeks and then came to our site to fill an opening as the Senior Logistician.

During my Tallit prayer, I asked God to *"**let the words of my mouth**, and the meditation of my heart, be acceptable in thy sight, O Lord, my strength, and my redeemer"* (Psalms 19:14). This helped me prepare for his arrival and be able to embrace him and speak life and positive things into his spirit. This scripture came to mind:

"A soft answer turneth away wrath: but grievous words stir up anger. The tongue of the wise useth knowledge aright: but the mouth of fools poureth out foolishness. The eyes of the LORD are in every place, beholding the evil and the good. A wholesome tongue is a tree of life: but perverseness therein is a breach in the spirit" (Proverbs 15:1-4).

6 June ~ "Before You Ask, I Will Answer"

I was busy conducting weekly maintenance on one of our vehicles, enjoying the opportunity to do something different and meaningful. Afterwards, I was craving something sweet for a snack. I really didn't want anything from the snack shop but decided to stop by just in case. While I was there, I stopped at the mail drop and, lo and behold, there was a package for me!

A co-worker, Myisha, sent me a care package. In it was exactly what I was craving…trail mix! I had to call her right away to thank her for thinking of me and also let her know that God answered my desire before I even asked for it.

I am so grateful that God continues to blow my mind with the small things!

"Delight thyself also in the LORD; and he shall give thee the desires of thine heart" (Psalms 37:4).

7 June ~ "Perseverance in the Midst of the Heat"

I saw this topic on my nephew Sammy's Facebook page. It was so relevant to what I have been going through. God had prepared me because the Senior Logistician was coming and it was certain that he would bring a lot of trouble with him. I knew this would be a test for me because I don't like dealing with foolishness. I like for the operation to run smoothly and for everyone to get along with each other.

Even though situations may get heated, I must push forward and not let problems or personalities cause me to sin. Satan is looking to push my buttons so I can fire off, but I must seek God to persevere through trials and become victorious!

"Fear none of those things which thou shalt suffer: behold, the devil shall cast some of you into prison, that ye may be tried; and ye shall have tribulation ten days: be thou faithful unto death, and I will give thee a crown of life" (Revelations 2:10).

8 June ~ "Military Tent Living"

Today is my youngest grandson Jayson's first birthday and his Naunna (the name used by my grandchildren to refer to me) is not there to share it with him. I was feeling a little down, but I didn't let myself dwell on that.

I'm really a soldier now—we're here in Herat at our other Compound and we have been assigned **housing in a military tent**. This tent is dark and creepy. The latrine is in another location, so we have to go around the corner and find the wooden building marked "Females." The latrine is one of the worst I've been in since deployed. The toilet stalls are really tight and the showers are old and yucky! Still, thank God for living conditions that are better than being outside on the ground.

There were two rows of six bunk beds in the tent, which reminded me of Camp Lightfoot. Camp Lightfoot is my church's campsite located in Williamsburg, Virginia. My husband and I served as counselors while our children attended camp there each summer. The tents in Herat had the same setup as Camp Lightfoot. The air conditioning unit was loud. It was pitch black at night. I was glad to have my trusty little flashlight. We had little four-legged visitors at night, so we slept with the light on for the remaining three nights. Four days and three nights in a tent weren't really that bad.

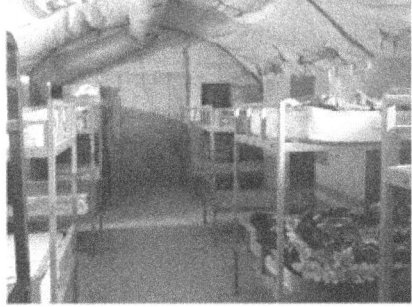

This experience made me think of Joseph in the Old Testament and Paul from the New Testament. Both were imprisoned under terrible conditions, much worse than mine. I actually became elated with the conditions that I found myself in, knowing that our soldiers were out on the battlefields, in tents or foxholes.

"Not that I speak in respect of want: for I have learned, in whatsoever state I am, therewith to be content. I know both how to be abased, and I know how to abound: everywhere and in all things I am instructed both to be full and to be hungry, both to abound and to suffer need. I can do all things through Christ which strengtheneth me" (Philippians 4:11-13).

9 June ~ "It Won't Fit"

This teachable moment came as I was watching the staff members in Herat trying to fit some exercise equipment through a door. It was quite comical. It took six men to take the equipment apart, turn it sideways, take the door off the building, etc. But **it just didn't fit!** They finally decided to put it in a connex (a large metal container used by the military to store or ship items) on the other side of the road, where it did fit.

How many times have we gone to the dressing room trying to make an outfit fit on our body when it is a size too small, only to make a final decision that **"it won't fit?"**

There are times that we try to fit one more appointment on the schedule, only to find that we've missed something else important due to overcrowding our lives with bad decisions. If we would only listen to God and let Him guide our paths, we could avoid unnecessary sorrows and headaches. **It won't fit**—some have learned that the hard way.

"Trust in the Lord with all thine heart; and lean not unto thine own understanding. In all thy ways acknowledge him, and he shall direct thy paths" (Proverbs 3:5-6).

10 June ~ "Lack of Support"

While making an assessment of the logistical needs at our Compound in Herat, I noticed the staff person had everything under control. She didn't need a full-time Logistician. I supposed that, but wanted to make a site visit to confirm my assessment; the HQ was not supporting me on this assessment. It was frustrating, because the support was needed elsewhere to a greater degree. Experiencing this lack of support from my HQ was distressing.

I thought about how Jesus must have felt when His disciples went to sleep while He was praying in the Garden of Gethsemane. Just as Christ forgave those who let Him down, we too must forgive when we don't get the support that we feel is necessary or expected from those around us. The **lack of support** from others will force us to trust and depend on God more.

My prayer is that God will help me not to complain about it, but trust Him to help me to get the job done! Even so, it gets frustrating when people in the church don't pull their weight and leave you hanging with all the work to do. Then when it comes time for recognition, they're the first up front as though they were the master contributor. "Fret not," I said to myself; "they will get their reward!"

My job is to humble myself, be patient and perform my tasks for God and not for man. Everything I say or do should be done to His glory and honor. I pray for focused direction as I want things to be done right. I do care about my responsibilities to ensure the best product is delivered.

"Rest in the LORD, and wait patiently for him: fret not thyself because of him who prospereth in his way, because of the man who bringeth wicked devices to pass. Cease from anger, and forsake wrath: fret not thyself in any wise to do evil" (Psalms 37:7-8).

11 June ~ "It's Hot as Hell"

Today was another beautiful day in Herat, Afghanistan! As I was sitting by the fire pit waiting to go into the office to check email, I noticed that my arms were on fire and were dark. I said to myself, "I'm toasted—**it's hot as hell** out here!"

We hear that term often referring to the weather. The sun here is fierce! I have sunscreen on, but I still got a dark tan. I'm now bronze on my arms and face. The wind was blowing which cooled me off, but when it stopped—**it's hot as hell**!

Is it really as hot here as it is in hell? Nope! Hell is a place reserved for the devil, his angels and those who will not repent and accept Jesus as Lord. Hell's fire is no match to what we experience by being out in the sun too long. Fire is hot! The sun beaming down on us is hot, but not even close to Hell's eternal burning fire.

I pray for any burn victim, that they'll never experience being in a fire or receive burning to their body again. Recognizing this should keep everyone out of Hell—only if they will repent and adhere to God's will for their lives. Give Hell its due props!

"For if God spared not the angels that sinned, but cast them down to hell, and delivered them into chains of darkness, to be reserved unto judgment;" (2 Peter 2:4).

11 June ~ "Never Alone"

I had a really great talk and worship time with one of the Reports Officers who is saved. We shared our thoughts and cried together. I encouraged her that God would not put any more on her than what she could bear. She needed to hear those words as comfort for she was feeling very lonely at this Compound. I encouraged her to use the extra time to spend with God as she was **not alone!** God has been with her throughout her deployment. I shared with her my journaling and outpouring of my heart to God in worship. These were the times that I was alone with God—in His presence.

I thank God for this experience of being here, living in this tent, using a bathroom and shower that were cruddy, not clean and not modern. Learning to be content and to do without the luxuries have made me appreciate my room at my Kabul Compound—not to mention my home—more than ever before. I want to appreciate everyone in a different way. I can't really express how I feel about the separation from home and everyone I know, but I am sure that I'll never take them for granted. Though I'm far away and miss my family greatly, I am **not alone**, for God is with me!

"Be strong and of a good courage, fear not, nor be afraid of them: for the LORD thy God, he it is that doth go with thee; he will not fail thee, nor forsake thee" (Deuteronomy 31:6).

12 June ~ "My Soul is Anchored"

During the flight to Kandahar, I took lots of pictures. I marveled as I observed the picturesque views of the mountains and valleys. God is the ultimate Artist, Designer and Creator. It is amazing how God designed the mountains to fit His pleasure. The valleys are anchored at the bottom of the mountains to provide greenery and a trench for free flowing water. Even though it is too dangerous to climb these mountains, I thank God for the opportunity to view them from the air—that's close enough for me!

I cried today, just thinking of Steve and Janelle Robinson, friends and fellow church members, as they begin the healing process due to the loss of Lisa. Steve was Lisa's husband and Janelle was her daughter. Lisa lost her battle to an inoperable tumor on 4 June 2012. I prayed for their spiritual health, that they would hold on to the anchor that they developed in the Lord.

I prayed that God would give me strength to make the anchor that I have launched even more secure. Satan will surely try to blow me off track, but during these storms, I must trust God to be my anchor. I know He'll lead me safely through any storm of life. I pray this as well for the Robinsons at this time.

"Which hope we have as an anchor of the soul, both sure and stedfast, and which entereth into that within the veil;" (Hebrews 6:19).

13 June ~ "I Hate to Wait"

We arrived at the helo pad in time to catch our flight to our other Compound in Kandahar, which is our most dangerous location. The flight was delayed…then delayed again…then delayed yet again. I really **hate to wait**, especially when I am on time. It is quite frustrating to me, but there was nothing I could do to make the helicopter show up.

Therefore, the lesson I learned today was: PATIENCE! Even though **I hate to wait**, waiting is a step in our growth process that must take place. "Lord, You know **I hate to wait**. I want things when I want them, I want to go somewhere or leave a place when I've planned to go or leave!"

Patience is a virtue and is not easily acquired. You have to go through something to get it. You learn to wait without complaining, even when it is uncomfortable. I watched the soldiers lie on the hard gravel, propped up by their backpacks, napping, and yet they didn't complain; they just waited for their flight. I thought, "Lord, help me to wait on You like the soldiers, so patiently, You are patient with me." My parents and family were patient with me as I developed into the woman God so delicately designed for me to be. **I hate to wait**, but must do so as I trust God for His timing.

"Be patient therefore, brethren, unto the coming of the Lord. Behold, the husbandman waiteth for the precious fruit of the earth, and hath long patience for it, until he receive the early and latter rain. Be ye also patient; stablish your hearts: for the coming of the Lord draweth nigh" (James 5:7-8).

14 June ~ "The Missed Opportunity"

I have to confess up front that I didn't adhere to my teachable moment yesterday. Patience awaited me but I missed it.

We were up early to check-in at the terminal at 0630 hours only to find out that it was the incorrect flight. We were told to come back at 1143 hours. We went back again, only to learn that our flight was cancelled. So, acting in the flesh, I was furious! To make me even madder, I found out that there was another flight that we could have taken at 1030 hours, but we were in the room watching TV.

I couldn't be mad with anyone but myself. When I was in the room watching TV, I heard helicopters flying in and flying out. A little small voice said, "Go check to see if it is your flight," but I ignored it. So there I was, waiting in the terminal for hours until a flight finally came at 1600 hours. Then, when it finally came, the plane only had room for the soldiers (they have first priority on the military flights). Being furious at this point, I grabbed my stuff and went back to the room.

After dinner, I checked in at the terminal and found out that the chopper that left at 1600 hours came back for us; unfortunately, because we weren't there, it left (again, without us). If I had only practiced the lesson that I heard yesterday and stayed in the terminal, I could have made the flight. But instead I chose to be angry and stubborn. I **missed the opportunity** to get back to the Kandahar Air Base today.

Therefore, my logistician and I had to wait until the next day to ride with the senior officers in up-armored vehicles, make the 45-minute trip on the most dangerous roadways in Afghanistan, and make our flight back to Kabul.

During my Tallit prayer time, I asked God for forgiveness for not practicing the lessons I've learned and for being disobedient to the Spirit which told me to GO! I may not have the patience of Job, but I will learn eventually to yield to the Spirit and walk in the path in which He wants me to trod.

"But they that wait on the LORD shall renew their strength; they shall mount up with wings as eagles; they shall run, and not be weary; and they shall walk, and not faint" (Isaiah 40:31).

"In your patience possess ye your souls" (Luke 21:19).

"And not only so, but we glory in tribulations also: knowing that tribulation worketh patience;" (Romans 5:3).

"For ye have need of patience, that, after ye have done the will of God, ye might receive the promise" (Hebrews 10:36).

15 June ~ "The Briefing"

Last night, we received a briefing from a British officer relating to our travel over the dangerous highways. I deliberated how detailed it was, the points he covered, every potential incident at various points on the trip, and alternate plans to implement if something happened. **The briefing** naturally caused me to suffer anxiety, but the Spirit quickly calmed my nerves. While listening to **the brief**, I prayed, asking God for protection.

Likewise, we too must prepare for our journey to heaven. We must calculate every possible issue and how to react to it. Satan has traps along this journey with the intent to kill, steal and destroy. We continually ask God for guidance and awareness of Satan's devices—that's why we need to put on the whole armor of God! My travel partner and I had to wear clothing to disguise our true posture and blend in. From a spiritual point of view, there is a contrast in **the briefing** we follow as Christians: we must be clothed in righteousness that will make us stand out in a crowd. The attention we want is for Jesus to be glorified and lifted up…so people who see us will be drawn to Christ, not us! If we follow the script which is the Word of God, God will go before us and make our route clear for passage. We arrived safely with no incidents (unlike the near death incident I experienced on March 22).

The people of God will arrive safely in heaven if we follow the guidance given in our "**Briefing**." The words of a song we sang in my home church gave me comfort: "I'll Press Along."

He goes before me and watches over me.
While on my journey, I'll press along.
He'll never forsake me.
My Savior will take me.
While on my journey, I'll press along. (Source Unknown)

"Only be strong and very courageous, that you may observe to do according to all the law which Moses My servant commanded you; do not turn from it to the right hand or to the left, that you may prosper wherever you go" (Joshua 1:7).

"I will bless the Lord who has given me counsel; My heart also instructs me in the night seasons. I have set the Lord always before me; Because He is at my right hand I shall not be moved. Therefore my heart is glad, and my glory rejoices; My flesh also will rest in hope" (Psalms 16:7-8).

15 June ~ "Ready for Home"

I have finished 80% of my deployment days and have just 20% more to go! Two more months and I'll be "home, sweet home." Each day I am getting more excited and as I prepare to pack and ship my stuff back, I am **ready for home**.

I was thinking about how good God has been to me during these four months. I still can't believe I'm doing this. Only through the grace of God am I actually accomplishing this adventurous goal. I learned today just how important home is to me. Sometimes you don't appreciate the water until the well is dry. I think I did appreciate home, but now I have the opportunity to appreciate it even more and not take my family or living in America for granted.

I'm also more excited about getting to my heavenly home. I have a fervent heart for God and my desire is to live so I can be home with Him to live forevermore!

"Lay not up for yourselves treasures upon earth, where moth and rust doth corrupt, and where thieves break through and steal: But lay up for yourselves treasures in heaven, where neither moth nor rust doth corrupt, and where thieves do not break through nor steal: For where your treasure is, there will your heart be also" (Matthew 6:19-21).

16 June ~ "Character Assassination"

I returned from my seven-day trip to a warm welcome from the staff—they said they really missed me.

Sometimes I think about my desire to make a difference and enhance the productivity of the support to this mission. I want to be part of the solution and see results and move this organization forward. I'll be quite disappointed if the projects I've started won't be completed prior to my departure. I've made a great impression on the leadership and staff here and am quite pleased that I had the opportunity to contribute. Because of my hard work, they would love for me to stay. (No way, I have to go home!)

I learned today that the Senior Logistician decided to file a complaint against me for **character assassination**. He felt that I spoke badly about him prior to his arrival. Far from the truth—his own leadership told me and my leadership that he was cantankerous and moody, but knew his stuff. I told them that we didn't have time for that type of attitude, but if he were to come, he would have to cooperate and become part of the team.

When we proclaim to be a Christian, say that we love and serve God, yet demonstrate something different than Christian ethics, we bring shame on the name of Jesus and the Body of Christ. Crucifying Christ afresh is definitely an act of **character assassination**. We cannot claim salvation and then still live in sin. By doing so, we proclaim that we don't believe Christ can keep us from falling into that sin again and again.

"For it is impossible for those who were once enlightened, and have tasted of the heavenly gift, and were made partakers of the Holy Ghost, And have tasted the good word of God, and the powers of the world to come, If they shall fall away, to renew them again unto repentance; seeing they crucify to themselves the Son of God afresh, and put him to an open shame" (Hebrews 6:4-6).

17 June ~ "Hard Knocks"

I spoke to my dad, Marion O'Connell Smith, Sr. and my husband, Frank to wish them a Happy Father's Day! I began thinking about the hard work my father performed for years in the dairy business. He learned the industry through lots of failures and lessons through **hard knocks**.

The lack of support from the HQ Logistics shop is really irritating me. At times, I want to throw my hands up and say, "FORGET IT!" I must be more patient, because sometimes others have to learn for themselves through **hard knocks**. I have to give them room to recognize that they've been misled. Yet, at the same time, I must never let things fall through the cracks.

This can make it difficult for me to stay engaged, but I won't give up. I won't let them spoil my great experience during this deployment. It has been a great learning opportunity and I've enjoyed working with the people here on the ground.

I don't plan to bump my head—I learn quickly! I've been there and refuse to go back. I did things the hard way and learned hard lessons. God gets no pleasure in my bumping my head against the wall. Life may be full of **hard knocks**, but the key is to count them as a learning experience and move forward.

"It is good for me that I have been afflicted; that I might learn thy statutes. The law of thy mouth is better unto me than thousands of gold and silver" (Psalms 119:71-72).

18 June ~ "Prepare for Game Day"

During my morning brief, I encouraged everyone to participate in the Compound Olympic Games on Friday. The team orchestrated tournaments for basketball, table tennis, pool, and horseshoes. People were out in full force today, practicing at their desired sport and getting ready for **game day**! I needed to practice on the ping pong table to get ready for my sport in the event.

The real **game day** for me, however, is the return of the Lord Jesus Christ. I have practiced and prepared throughout the years to ensure my spiritual body is fit and rapture-ready. I will need to keep practicing to stay sharp for that day.

"Know ye not that they which run in a race run all, but one receiveth the prize? So run, that ye may obtain" (1 Corinthians 9:24).

19 June ~ "Accepting His Will"

I learned last week that I received a job offer from my former boss. Even though I prayed for a promotion, this job was not a promotion. It was a job performing similar executive officer duties—nothing challenging, but I would also assist with establishing a new office. The latter was exciting enough for me to say yes.

Accepting God's will for me to agree to this position was evident. I didn't have to apply for the job. He told me that I was the first person he thought of to help him establish this new office. Plus, the job is located in the Pentagon. I used to dream of working in the Pentagon when I was young. When my parents drove us to Washington, DC to see my Aunt Madge, we would pass the Pentagon on Interstate 395. Thus, a previous dream is fulfilled.

It is awesome to be thought of in this manner. God knows what's best and in His perfect will and time He will bless me with a promotion. "Thank You God!"

"Rejoice evermore. Pray without ceasing. In everything give thanks: for this is the will of God in Christ Jesus concerning you. Quench not the Spirit" (1 Thessalonians 5:16-19).

20 June ~ "Spiritual Gifts"

We had an awesome Bible study on **spiritual gifts** tonight! It is important to know where one fits in the Body of Christ. I learned so much from the attendees as to where they thought they were gifted. You can think you know people; but, you really don't know what God has put in someone's spirit to do until you specifically speak about it. One of the Reports Officers is gifted in cooking and making people happy as their bellies get full—this talent demonstrates her gift of hospitality. She has been so helpful to us on the Compound. She gets in the kitchen and throws down a great meal. Everyone raved about her baked beans! One person said, "Those baked beans were so good; they'll make you wanna smack your mother!" I don't eat beans, but tried her potato salad and thoroughly enjoyed it. Yes, she is gifted with the preparation of food.

I ask God continually to use me as an instrument for His glory and honor. I have the gift of administration and enjoy using it to enhance the church and my organization where I work. I am sure He has blessed others through the gift He has placed inside of me.

"As every man hath received the gift, even so minister the same one to another, as good stewards of the manifold grace of God" (1 Peter 4:10).

127

21 June ~ "The Free Gift"

I went to our other site today—shopping of course! Yes, I was also there to conduct business. We cleaned the shelves of basic cell phones from the electronics store. The store manager gave us **free** phone cards to go with our cell phones. The vendor where I shopped gave me some **free** stuff because I purchased several items from him. I mentioned to the staff that accompanied me that it was nice for the vendor to do that; I wasn't expecting the **free gifts**.

Jesus paid the price for our sins on the cross. He gave His life **freely**, just as the vendor gave from his inventory **freely**. It is so much more appreciated when someone gives you a **free gift** that you didn't expect to get. We should not expect anything as if we deserve it; we really don't deserve anything on this Earth. But, because the penalty for our death sentence was paid in full, we get to walk away from sin and be at peace with our decision to worship and believe in God.

I encourage you to thank God for **the free gift** of His Son Jesus!

"For God so loved the world, that he gave his only begotten Son, that whosoever believeth in him should not perish, but have everlasting life" (John 3:16).

22 June ~ "Dealing with Adult Children"

Okay, Lord, my spirit is vexed right now! Help! I had it out with my First Sergeant about pulling his weight with oversight duties at the Vehicle Maintenance Facility (VMF) site. He whined like a kid and threw a temper tantrum, storming out of the office. Of course, I don't have time for this petty stuff. I told him he would go to provide oversight at the VMF as everyone else who shared this responsibility! (He did.)

I thought about God and how He feels when we act like children and refuse to do our part in the building of His kingdom. Sometimes people come up with all kinds of reasons for not pulling their weight. "I'm tired. I've got something else to do. Why do I have to do it all the time? Call Sister or Brother so and so, they are better at that job." Endless whining…

He said in His Word that we should eat the meat of the Word and yet we whine for milk. We are no longer supposed to be bottle-fed. We are exhorted to grow up and be productive members of the Body of Christ. We must stop acting like children!

Lord, have mercy on us!

"And he said, If now I have found grace in thy sight, O LORD, let my LORD, I pray thee, go among us; for it is a stiffnecked people; and pardon our iniquity and our sin, and take us for thine inheritance" (Exodus 34:9).

"The hand of the diligent shall bear rule: but the slothful shall be under tribute" (Proverbs 12:24).

"As the door turneth upon his hinges, so doth the slothful upon his bed" (Proverbs 26:14).

"That ye be not slothful, but followers of them who through faith and patience inherit the promises" (Hebrews 6:12).

23 June ~ "What Day, What Hour?"

I had to make the dangerous road trip to Bagram today. Sometimes when I go off the Compound, I wonder, is this the day that He wants me to come home to Heaven? The answer has always been, NO! Not that I'm longing to go right now; but I am just being curious!

No man knows the **day** or **hour** that the Son of God will return for us. Thank God for that! We have so many false preachers claiming that they know the answer. If they were true believers, they would denounce that notion and submit to God's Word which says that *"even the angels don't know."* What makes anyone think that God will select him or her to know when Jesus does not know?

What we actually need to know is where we stand with God at every moment. We must live so that whenever it is our time to go, we won't be ashamed or unready for His coming. Then we will not be so concerned about **what day** or **what hour** He will come!

"But of that day and that hour knoweth no man, no, not the angels which are in heaven, neither the Son, but the Father" (Mark 13:32).

129

24 June ~ "Unfinished Projects"

As I was leaving the Vehicle Maintenance Facility (VMF) construction site, I thought about how anxious I was to see this project finished before I return to the states. We've had so many stops and hindrances that it will be impossible to finish by August. The engineer sent by HQ has slowed the construction.

I'd like to see this construction project and several other **unfinished projects** completed prior to my departure. Some are not make-or-break projects, but are just some improvements to the processes and procedures.

Often we feel pressured to get stuff done before a major event, trip, vacation, wedding, death, or even leaving for the day. Spiritually, there are some things I want to accomplish; more witnessing, and getting someone to draw closer to God. Not so much to make a mark, but because it was a desire and prime purpose for being here. Before we leave this Earth, we should have urgency about winning souls for Christ! Why? Because Satan is busy and the harvest is plentiful. An **unfinished project of soul-winning is** important and should be placed high on the priority list. We want God's kingdom to grow to His glory.

I've shared my testimony/story with many people, Afghan and Americans, and pray that God will count this sharing as contribution to the great mission.

"But none of these things move me, neither count I my life dear unto myself, so that I might finish my course with joy, and the ministry, which I have received of the Lord Jesus, to testify the gospel of the grace of God" (Acts 20:24).

25 June ~ "Put Your Clothes on First"

As I was getting ready for the day, I reminded myself that I am living in a situation where I need to rethink even the most normal of chores. I remembered not to lag around in the bathroom without prioritizing getting my **clothes on first** before doing other things. The reason is that if there was an emergency, brushing my teeth could wait. I can't run out the door with my helmet and weapons if I don't have on my clothes.

In the same way, we need to remind ourselves that in our spiritual battle, we must first be clothed in righteousness each day. Our breastplate should be on so that we can be ready in an instant to respond to the enemy of our souls. **Put your clothes on first** thing after the cleansing of your bodies and souls!

"Wherefore take unto you the whole armour of God that ye may be able to withstand in the evil day, and having done all, to stand. Stand therefore, having your loins girt about with truth, and having on the breastplate of righteousness; And your feet shod with the preparation of the gospel of peace; Above all, taking the shield of faith, wherewith ye shall be able to quench all the fiery darts of the wicked. And take the helmet of salvation, and the sword of the Spirit, which is the word of God: Praying always with all prayer and supplication in the Spirit, and watching thereunto with all perseverance and supplication for all saints;" (Ephesians 6:13-18).

"I will greatly rejoice in the LORD, my soul shall be joyful in my God; for he hath clothed me with the garments of salvation, he hath covered me with the robe of righteousness, as a bridegroom decketh himself with ornaments, and as a bride adorneth herself with her jewels" (Isaiah 61:10).

26 June ~ "He Goes Before Me"

Today I was amazed how God **goes before me** and paves the way for His will for my life. I was talking to my previous boss about the job he wants me to take when I return. In speaking with my current boss, he was excited for me and said he would do whatever was needed to make it happen.

Sometimes, if we just get out of the way and let God work on our behalf, things will work much more smoothly. "Thank you, Lord, for working things out on my behalf without my asking."

"And it shall come to pass, that before they call, I will answer; and while they are yet speaking, I will hear" (Isaiah 65:24).

27 June ~ "When There're No Saints Around"

I worked the Command Quarters (CQ) shift last night into this morning. Thank God everything was safe and calm while I was on CQ duty. As I was preparing for my nap, I was thinking about the saints at my home church and how I missed them.

Out here, I'm away from all that I know to be true, honest, and loving; my fellow saints. There are some saved folks here, but there's nothing like relationships you have with the saints you know well!

I thought about how important it was for us to live godly lives in front of our families and church body. What we hear and learn from each other can really benefit and edify others. I think of Sister Cilly Brooks, as she always testified about her previous times in the mental institution away from her family and not even knowing anybody. **No saints were around** her then. But someone prayed for her—that person had her on their mind and took a little time to pray for her. I pray for Sister Cilly Brooks now: "God, grant her the desires of her heart for her children to be saved. Give her what she needs to be a light for you. Grant the pardon for her son who's in prison." From her consistent testimony, I've learned: "He may not come when you want Him, but He's always right on time—you can't hurry God, you just have to wait!"

I admire Sister Ruthie Thornton's (another saint at home) encouragement during her testimony: "I pray that my faith won't fail me, and Work the Word!"

Another saint, Sister Ernestine Smith, has a testimony and favorite song entitled, "I Will Abide" that are inspirations to me:

> *I will abide in all God's ways,*
> *His way is best, I do not doubt.*
> *He may not give me what I ask,*
> *But He gives me grace to do without.* (Source Unknown)

Sister Grace Davis' favorite testimony was: "If we ever needed the Lord before we sure do need Him now."

I depend on the lives and words of encouragement of these saints for survival. Sometimes the Word of God doesn't come to my mind but I will remember the testimonies of the saints. I appreciate the saints even more so because **they are not around.**

But I need what they so freely share—experience and encouragement.

It is so important to live your life so someone can get something out of it. They can learn and depend on what you so freely share—even **when you're not around**. "Lord, let my light shine so others may be enlightened by the words of my mouth."

"And they that be wise shall shine as the brightness of the firmament; and they that turn many to righteousness as the stars for ever and ever" (Daniel 12:3).

28 June ~ "Just When You Need Him"

When I arrived in the office today, I was searching for the Communications Technician. I was frustrated because when I needed him, he was not available. Why does it seem like when you need assistance from someone, they're not around or available? But, when you don't need them, they're right there in your face! Shopping is an example. Sales people are always asking you, "Can I help you with something?" when you don't need them. But, when you REALLY need them, they're nowhere to be found!

Thank God, Jesus is always there, even when He may not seem to come right when you want Him. But there are times when you cry out and He's right there at that moment of need. An example would be if you are driving through an intersection and a car runs the red light and you scream, "JESUS!" Then He maneuvers the vehicle out of your path! He was right there, **just when you needed Him**.

God is *not* like the salesperson that's being a pest to you all day, but when the need arises, He's right there, on time! We serve a faithful God who tends to the needs of His children. What a loving Father. I'm thankful for another day of God's protection.

"God is our refuge and strength, a very present help in trouble. Therefore will not we fear, though the earth be removed, and though the mountains be carried into the midst of the sea" (Psalms 46:1-2).

29 June ~ "Promises Not Kept"

I was musing on the promises made by HQ and how they reneged on those promises. The Logistics Chief had promised to backfill the facility manager position as soon as possible. We experienced several issues with our water supply and kitchen sanitation because we lost the top-notch facility manager that HQ fired due to a personality conflict. It was a true morale-buster. You can lose confidence in someone's word when the people you depend on to support you constantly fail in providing support. It is heartbreaking at times and I must confess that I'm not quite over HQ's lack of support yet. I pray that God will help me to heal and forgive those who made **promises not kept**.

I am so glad that God is true to His word. He said, *"...it shall not return unto me void, but it shall accomplish that which I please, and it shall prosper in the thing whereto I sent it."* (Isaiah 55:11). He is faithful to fulfill any promise. He has never failed me. I'll keep on trusting His Word and living so that He is glorified.

I get excited when I see Him at work in the lives of my family and myself. When I'm going through a trial or disappointment, I must also get excited about how God plans to work it out. It is an act of faith. "Lord, help my lack of excitement during these times."

"The Lord is not slack concerning his promise, as some men count slackness; but is longsuffering to us-ward, not willing that any should perish, but that all should come to repentance" (2 Peter 3:9).

30 June ~ "When There're No Refreshments"

Whew—it was a hot one today! I had to get up early to do the water run with the Commander. We drove the "soft skin" van, which has no armor, to our other site to pick up the necessary water for the Compound. The traffic was heavy and we had a few close calls. The Commander had a little struggle with the manual shifting. I tried not to laugh, but it was difficult not to at least snicker a little.

We packed two pallets of water into the van. I pulled a muscle in my shoulder with all the lifting and throwing the packs of water. After we finished, we both were hot and tired. I went to the Green Beans coffee shop to get a cold, icy smoothie to soothe my drought condition and quench my thirst. But, they had none available. In addition, the little juice shop that I often frequented was CLOSED! So I couldn't get my cranberry-kiwi drink that I like.

I was hot and tired from all the work, but everywhere I went to get refreshment, I came up dry. How discouraging and devastating! "Lord have mercy, I'm going to die in this wilderness from thirst!" **No Refreshments**! Of course, we did have a van loaded with water, so what was the problem?

When we go to church or attend a service, seeking a refreshing word and don't receive it, we can get discouraged. The Bible speaks of a time when it will be hard to go to where the Word is being preached. Therefore, we must eat, digest and study God's Word so it will be in our hearts and minds when we need refreshing but nothing is available. It is a very DRY place when you can't get a refreshing from God's Word or His people.

According to Matthew 5:6, *"Blessed are they which do hunger and thirst after righteousness: for they shall be filled."* God's Word will give you the refreshing substance to sustain you as you go throughout the day.

"And Jesus said unto them, I am the bread of life: he that cometh to me shall never hunger; and he that believeth on me shall never thirst" (John 6:35).

JULY 2012

1 July ~ "Non-potable Water"

While in Afghanistan, we have been directed not to drink the faucet water or use it to brush our teeth. The cooks are not to cook with the water from the public system. We see signs on water trucks that read "**non-potable water.**"

Thank God there is a fountain that we can drink from freely; it is a fountain of living water that shall never run dry. It is the living water of Jesus Christ flowing from the Father. This water will sustain and strengthen us from day to day.

We should be careful to only drink from a pure source. Even though water may look clean, there could be contaminants that could make us sick due to poor sanitation procedures. We should judge all other water by the living water from Jesus. This water from Christ is not only good for us, but it provides everlasting life. Jesus is the living, drinkable water!

"But whosoever drinketh of the water that I shall give him shall never thirst; but the water that I shall give him shall be in him a well of water springing up into everlasting life" (John 4:14).

1 July ~ "Ah, That Tastes Good"

I've learned through experience that not everything that **tastes good** is *good* for you. While deployed, it was essential for me to ensure my immune system was replenished with Vitamin C and other nutrients daily. The vitamins I brought along with me did not have a pleasant taste, but I'd made it thus far with only getting sick once.

Prior to my deployment, I purchased Sunny Maid Vitamin C chewable tablets, which I'd used for years. However, I noticed that my grocery store no longer carried this brand of Vitamin C. I was disappointed as I preferred this brand over all others due to the great orange **taste**. I did some research and found that one of the ingredients was known to cause cancer and that is why stores began to remove the product from their shelves. But it **tasted so good**!

Sin can also **taste really good** while systematically killing you both spiritually and physically. Let sin go and get the delicious **taste** of the Word of God. It will benefit you physically and, most importantly, spiritually!

"How sweet are thy words unto my taste! Yea, sweeter than honey to my mouth!" (Psalms 119:103).

2 July ~ "Standing in the Gap"

Today I played referee between my Lead Mechanic and Facility Engineer regarding space at the Vehicle Maintenance Facility site. The Lead Mechanic felt the new design of the facility would not allow enough space for the ingress and egress of vehicles in and out of the gate. The Facility Engineer was sticking to his concept design. Because the situation became elevated, I stepped in with a compromise that they both could agree on.

The Lead Mechanic wanted a design with space to park the vehicles in front of the facility. The Facility Engineer designed a more narrow space in front of the facility to be used as a driveway with no space for parking. I redrew the sketch, moving the generators on the outside of the main facility to allow for parking the vehicles in a space closer to the gate, but still within the protected fence. We discussed this layout and they both agreed to the new plan. We discussed the importance of looking at the plans at different angles to maximize the usage of the square footage allotted for the project.

As Christians, we are called to be peacemakers. I love it when God gives me a solution to address man's problems, especially when **standing in the gap** results in peace!

"Blessed are the peacemakers: for they shall be called the children of God" (Matthew 5:9).

3 July ~ "When He Calls Me"

Not everyone subscribes to the notion that, when God calls you to do something for Him, you'll answer to your name. Sometimes when He calls, you may come kicking and screaming, but you'll eventually be where He wants you to be.

Don't get me wrong, God gives us free will to choose, but His will is always accomplished, whether through you or someone else. It pays to comply without heartache, pain, or misery. It is useless to kick against the pricks of your conscience.

The words of the song entitled, **"When He Calls Me"** were ringing in my heart tonight:

> *When He calls me, I will answer.*
> *When He calls me, I will answer to my name.*
> *I'll be somewhere working on my soul salvation,*
> *When He calls my name.* (Source Unknown)

The keyword is "working." I want Him to find me working **when He calls me**.

"And he called his ten servants, and delivered them ten pounds, and said unto them, Occupy till I come" (Luke 19:13).

4 July ~ "It's Your Birthday"

Today is my firstborn's 32nd birthday. Happy Birthday Christina! Even though I'm far away from you, I can still reach out from Afghanistan and wish you a blessed and enjoyable day!

God gives us a new start and new mercies every day. Each day should be celebrated the same way you celebrate a birthday. Birth is newness to life. God breathes life into us daily. We will never see today again, so give it your fullest attention; rejoice and celebrate!

"And the LORD God formed man [of] the dust of the ground, and breathed into his nostrils the breath of life; and man became a living soul." (Genesis 2:7).

5 July ~ "The Speck in My Eye"

How irritating … I had to get the contact out of my right eye because it was causing me great discomfort. I performed the eye wash routine, but my eye was still irritated.

Spiritually, we have **specks in our own eyes** and lives that should be addressed prior to trying to get someone else straight. We need eye salve to heal and remove the irritants inside ourselves. Otherwise, we will continue in a self-righteous state of mind.

Once we know the issues we have, the Word of God is the balm that opens our understanding and helps us remove our shortcomings. Get yourself right first so you can see clearly; then, what you thought was a speck in someone else's eye may not be a speck at all.

"Judge not, that ye be not judged. For with what judgment ye judge, ye shall be judged: and with what measure ye mete, it shall be measured to you again. And why beholdest thou the mote that is in thy brother's eye, but considerest not the beam that is in thine own eye? Or how wilt thou say to thy brother, Let me pull out the mote out of thine eye; and, behold, a beam is in thine own eye? Thou hypocrite, first cast out the beam out of thine own eye; and then shalt thou see clearly to cast out the mote out of thy brother's eye" (Matthew 7:1-5).

6 July ~ "Fake Tears"

I had a discussion with my Junior Logistician. She was frustrated about how her supervisor at HQ was treating her. She began to shed some tears.

My inner voice said, "Oh please, spare me and stop the drama!" From my two months of observing her work and personality, I knew they were forced tears.

God knows our hearts, thoughts, and motives. You can fool some people, but you can't fool God. **Fake tears** will not move God. When you get in trouble, don't cry and whine when you know it was your own fault that got you in that situation.

As Christians, we are also to have compassion on those who are going through hardships or difficulty, whether it is of their own doings or the undertaking of someone else. "God help me to have compassion on others, even when they are displaying **fake tears**!"

"Rejoice with them that do rejoice, and weep with them that weep" (Romans 12:15).

6 July ~ "Push Us Out"

"Push us out" is a term that is used to extend the time of an operation. When we are off the Compound and our mission extends past the time we posted on the tracking board, we must call into Command Quarters to let them know we need more time.

Sometimes we feel that we need more time to complete missions for God. There are so many souls to reach, so many that need a healing, so many that need help. We have family members that need to know the Lord. God knows and will extend our time so we can complete the mission.

God dropped this prayer in my spirit while I was away from the Compound. "Lord, I know my father is ailing and longs to be with You, but please extend his time until I return home. I have been faithful to You, Oh God, and ask of You this petition. He has more great-grandchildren to see, hold and take pictures with; he has more stories of God's love to share with his family. Therefore, Lord, push Dad out. Give him more time on the clock. His desire (and mine) is to be in the land of the living when I get home from Afghanistan. So, Lord, please **'Push Him Out!'**"

"Then Hezekiah turned his face toward the wall, and prayed unto the LORD, And said, Remember now, O LORD, I beseech thee, how I have walked before thee in truth and with a perfect heart, and have done that which

is good in thy sight. And Hezekiah wept sore. Then came the word of the LORD to Isaiah, saying, Go, and say to Hezekiah, Thus saith the LORD, the God of David thy father, I have heard thy prayer, I have seen thy tears: behold, I will add unto thy days fifteen years. And I will deliver thee and this city out of the hand of the king of Assyria: and I will defend this city. And this shall be a sign unto thee from the LORD that the LORD will do this thing that he hath spoken; Behold, I will bring again the shadow of the degrees, which is gone down in the sun dial of Ahaz, ten degrees backward. So the sun returned ten degrees, by which degrees it was gone down" (Isaiah 38:2–8).

7 July ~ "Hot Temper"

It was a hot day today. I became overheated at the Vehicle Maintenance Facility construction site, so I poured water over my head and neck—boy did that do the trick!

I talked to my daughter Christina and she shared the issues she was having with her son Isaiah at school with his **hot temper**. I prayed that God would help him to think before he acted or shouted out loud. I prayed for a cooling of his **hot temper**! As adults, we need to mind our tongues and not let anger lay heavy on our hearts. It will only lead to a disaster if untreated.

"Be not hasty in thy spirit to be angry: for anger resteth in the bosom of fools" (Ecclesiastes 7:9).

8 July ~ "Metal-Against-Metal"

I cleaned my M-11 9mm handgun with the assistance of our senior officer. Later, I had one of my Operations Support Team members check it. He previously served as a Marine combat soldier, losing an eye to the enemy's Improvised Explosive Device (IED). He went to Individual Protective Measures Training with me last year, and was a qualified range instructor. He loves guns and takes his apart daily for cleaning and inspection. After examining it, he told me my weapon didn't have enough oil, and that **metal against metal** could cause a jam.

I thought about why we have so much friction between each other as people—we are like **metal against metal**. We often bump heads because of the lust of our flesh. We all want to have things our way, making sparks fly everywhere!

That's why we need the anointing of the Holy Spirit. We need the holy oil that will smooth our edges and rough spots so we'll be calm and agreeable. Get some Holy Ghost oil and apply it daily!

"Thou hast loved righteousness, and hated iniquity; therefore God, even thy God, hath anointed thee with the oil of gladness above thy fellows" (Hebrews 1:9).

9 July ~ "Are You Overweight?"

I was weighing myself, as I do every night and morning, and God revealed this teachable moment.

We are often weighed down with the burdens from the cares of this life. We need to get on the spiritual scale and see just how much **we are overweight** due to the heavy load in our lives. The Word of God is our scale. As we read and digest the Word, it will help us to lose the weight of iniquity so that we'll be fit for the Master's use. Let's lose some weight today and keep it off.

Are you overweight?

"Come unto me, all ye that labour and are heavy laden, and I will give you rest. Take my yoke upon you, and learn of me; for I am meek and lowly in heart: and ye shall find rest unto your souls" (Matthew 11:28-29).

10 July ~ "You Can't Always Be Right"

It took me about two and half hours to respond to an email I received from the HQ logistics folk. I had to remove and rewrite some thoughts because I wanted them to be received in the spirit in which I uttered them. These folk seem to be trying to vex my spirit. I hate to see others being wronged by leadership. I don't take too well to inaccurate and unfounded accusations.

I've always stood up for myself and never let anyone run over or take advantage of me. I just need to let God stand up for me and not fret with unknowledgeable people and sometimes those who are evildoers. I am confident in my abilities and when I see wrong, I call it out!

"Speak to me, Holy Ghost. No Robyn, **you can't always be right**! But when you are, please treat the spiteful abusers with love, and be confident in knowing *inside* that you're **right**. You don't always have to verbally communicate: 'I'm right!' Having that reaction may not seem fair, but life is not always fair … so get over it!"

"Fret not thyself because of evil men, neither be thou envious at the wicked: For there shall be no reward to the evil man; the candle of the wicked shall be put out" (Proverbs 24:19-20).

10 July ~ "Physical Forgiveness"

I have had an issue with one of my staff members being abusive to others. He did apologize for statements he made in an email to me. Even though I didn't harbor any unforgiveness in my heart against him, I just needed to get to the point of **physical forgiveness**. **Forgiveness** is a process.

We can speak with our mouths or write it down that we forgive, but until you demonstrate **forgiveness**, you really have not forgiven. "Help me Holy Ghost! Show me; let me know what I need to do and how to do it. In the name of Jesus, this is your servant's prayer."

"Let all bitterness, and wrath, and anger, and clamour, and evil speaking, be put away from you, with all malice: And be ye kind one to another, tenderhearted, forgiving one another, even as God for Christ's sake hath forgiven you" (Ephesians 4:31-32).

11 July ~ "Just for Who You Are"

I was in a worship mode this morning, thanking God for just being God. How often do we appreciate God and let Him know it? We tend to be busy asking for things and forget who we're talking to. He is the Almighty God, He gave us the Prince of Peace, the Lily of the Valley and Bright and Morning Star. He is the Great "I Am." He is God Jehovah… and therefore, He is worthy to be praised. All honor and glory belongs to Him.

"Lord, I just wanted to take a moment to worship You in my writing today, **just for who You are!**"

"But the hour cometh, and now is, when the true worshippers shall worship the Father in spirit and in truth: for the Father seeketh such to

worship him. God is a Spirit: and they that worship him must worship him in spirit and in truth" (John 4:23-24).

12 July ~ "I'll Be With You"

While at the Vehicle Maintenance Facility construction site today, I got a picture of a desert dragon that was hurt during construction. This lizard is often found in places like Afghanistan. Their color is similar to the sand, making it easy for them to hide. WOW! I guess God was with him—he survived the injury.

I returned to the Compound and was sitting at my desk in my room when the water bottle on the desk started rocking back and forth. We were having an earthquake! I waited a few minutes and then inspected the buildings with the Senior Logistician. No major damage.

I began to think of the goodness of God's grace and protection. **He was with me** during the Vehicle Borne Improvised Explosive Device (VBIED) explosion, a previous earthquake, the fire in the workshop, and now this earthquake. God said **He would be with me**. And I want to say, "Thank You!"

"...And lo, I am with you always, even unto the end of the world" (Matthew 28:20b).

13 July ~ "Children at Play"

While checking the monitors on Command Quarters (CQ) night duty, I was watching the Afghan children and young men playing stick ball in the street outside our Compound. These innocent young people were having a great time, not knowing what was going on inside our Compound. I wanted so badly to give them some of our sports equipment to show that we cared, but we are not allowed to do that. We do throw their balls back over the wall when they accidentally fly over.

If we could only be as those **children at play**, enjoying one another, with seemingly no cares in the world, this world would be in a better place. We should have a child-like heart when dealing with one another, forgiving and easy to get along with. We are to build up and comfort those around us as an act of worship.

"And said, Verily I say unto you, Except ye be converted, and become as little children, ye shall not enter into the kingdom of heaven. Whosoever therefore shall humble himself as this little child, the same is greatest in the kingdom of heaven" (Matthew 18:3-4).

13 July ~ "Consider the Ant"

While at the Vehicle Maintenance Facility construction site, I was sitting in the chair, focusing on the ground when I noticed a colony of ants. They were always busy, never seeming to rest nor sleep. They were building their homes, finding food, and bumping into each other without fighting!

The ant can accomplish so much with so little, and can carry items twice its size. Why do we find it so hard to get along while at work? Why do we complain and get weary about going to work each day? Stop, think, and **"consider the ant."**

"Go to the ant, thou sluggard; consider her ways, and be wise: Which having no guide, overseer, or ruler, Provideth her meat in the summer, and gathereth her food in the harvest" (Proverbs 6:6-8).

14 July ~ "Packing Up—Mission Accomplished"

Thirty Days Remaining!

As I stand here looking at the items I need to pack, I'm saddened to leave. The past five months have been a great learning experience. I so appreciate the gift of health and strength granted by my almighty and loving God to show me how much He loves me. It has been a privilege to be here amongst the people of Afghanistan.

I must now prepare my belongings to ship home, things that I so carefully selected to bring here to ensure I felt the comforts of home. Now these things will go back with me, forever to remind me of the comfort they provided while I was in Afghanistan alone. Pictures of my grandsons—looking so handsome, smiling— brought me so much comfort! Having my own communion set to partake monthly was special! It hurt me so to leave my wedding rings, but I did bring the ring Frank gave me as my Valentine's Day gift on the day I left. I wore it on a chain around my neck daily. That brought me a sense of peace and resolve. I know our relationship will be better and lasting. Distance does make the heart grow fonder. We have so much to share when I get home.

Packing brings back memories of all the stuff I wanted to bring because I thought I would need it, only to find out after getting here that I didn't need it after all. **Packing** makes me happy, excited, and fulfilled. I feel complete.

I went through the battle of training and lectures to get here and by the grace of God, I **completed the mission**. I worked hard (through the dangers of VBIEDs and other unseen dangers) to make this environment a little better for the people I served while here. I'm proud of my accomplishments and give all the credit, honor, and glory to God. Without His divine grace, mercy, guidance, and direction, I could not have been successful. I live to worship and give honor and glory to His Name, for He alone is worthy of all the praise!

No matter how much I write in this journal, I cannot express how I really feel about the grace and mercy bestowed upon me while here. I will forever pray and be confident that my being here accomplished what His plan was for me and that Jesus Christ was demonstrated through word or deed to those I came in contact with.

Packing up reminds me that I have more places to go and more people to reach. "Thank You Lord for the opportunity to '**pack up!**' WHAT'S NEXT?"

"Being confident of this very thing, that he which hath begun a good work in you will perform it until the day of Jesus Christ:" (Philippians 1:6).

14 July ~ "Is Thine Heart Right"

After taking a nap following my Command Quarters (CQ) nightshift, I got to the office to learn that one of our senior officers was medevac'd to the Kabul International Airport Hospital for chest pains and potential heart issues. I spent the next two hours tracking him down to ensure we knew where he was and so that we could be informed of his condition. I told our Operations Support Team Lead to let him know that I was praying for him.

As a result of this incident, God dropped this in my spirit. Now is the day of salvation, not tomorrow. Tomorrow is not promised. We don't know when we'll check out; therefore, it pays to be right and live right so that you'll die right. Get a checkup and answer this question: **"Is thine heart righ**t with God?"

"(For he saith, I have heard thee in a time accepted, and in the day of salvation have I succoured thee: behold, now is the accepted time; behold, now is the day of salvation)" (2 Corinthians 6:2).

15 July ~ "Humble Me"

In the Department of Defense, it is customary for employees to draft their own evaluations and award nominations, since you're the only one who *really* knows what you've done to accomplish the mission. After you've submitted your evaluation and nomination(s), your supervisor is responsible for writing and submitting the award. My Commander told me I was too humble in my write-up for my award. I said, "Thanks—fix it up!" I felt bad that I had to write it because I didn't want to give the impression that I was being boastful. I know who enabled me to be successful in the things that I accomplished—God!

"Humble me" Lord so I may do Your will!

"Humble yourselves in the sight of the Lord, and he shall lift you up." (James 4:10)

"Humble yourselves therefore under the mighty hand of God, that he may exalt you in due time:" (1 Peter 5:6).

16 July ~ "Thanks and Goodbye"

After mailing my first foot locker home, I felt really good and excited. I have a little more shopping to do for a few special folks, like my friend Doris "California" Coates. She was close to my heart during my time here—she sent cards for each month to encourage me, and I want to say, **"Thanks!"**

Today was my initial Commander's last day. I gave him a big hug as we all ceremonially saw him off to the airport. As a Marine Colonel, he was very level-headed. I know some that are Type A to the "T." I so enjoyed working under his leadership. He was a great boss! Saying **goodbye** was hard, but necessary—he had another assignment to go to.

We all must say **goodbye** at some point as we move on to bigger and better things. We say hello and **goodbye** to each day that comes and passes. Each day given to us is a day that we've never seen before and will never see again.

Thank God there are loved ones and believers that **we'll thank** for their service and love toward us. When we must say **goodbye** to them, we have confidence that we'll see them again in the rapture and forever when we get to heaven.

"Then we which are alive and remain shall be caught up together with them in the clouds, to meet the Lord in the air: and so shall we ever be with the Lord" (1 Thessalonians 4:17).

17 July ~ "Peach Smoothie"

It was another beautiful, hot day in Afghanistan. God has truly blessed us with good weather—yes, we've had some hot days, but the nights and evenings are cooler. While at one of our other sites, I was really craving a smoothie. I normally get the strawberry flavor, but decided to try the **peach flavored smoothie**. Much to my surprise, it hit the spot and quenched my thirst. Sometimes we miss out on something good just because we've never tried it before and that fear kept us in the dark on how good it could be.

The relationship that we develop with God will ensure everlasting life that will quench our thirst for righteousness. People miss out on a powerful relationship for fear of the unknowns of God. How will they get to know Him if we don't tell them? I'm reminded of the story of the Samaritan woman who met Jesus at the well (John 4:7-14). After her encounter with Christ, she was not afraid to share her story with others. Because of her boldness, many other Samaritans sought Him out and became believers.

Share your story about the **peach smoothie** experience. Let the world know just how good God is to you, how He saved you from your wrongdoings, how you believe that Jesus died on the cross to pay the sin and death penalty, and how you no longer are a servant to sin, but a member of the Body of Christ.

"And many of the Samaritans of that city believed on him for the saying of the woman, which testified, He told me all that ever I did. So when the Samaritans were come unto him, they besought him that he would tarry with them: and he abode there two days. And many more believed because of his own word; And said unto the woman, Now we believe, not because of thy saying: for we have heard him ourselves, and know that this is indeed the Christ, the Saviour of the world" (John 4:39-42).

18 July ~ "Failure is Not an Option"

Today I was sharing with my new Commander how God has my life all planned out. I told him about the teachable moments God gives to me each day. He responded that we all can learn something new each day and thought these moments were a special gift for me.

God has been good to me in allowing me this time alone with Him. God has never failed me. He's my keeper and protector. This is an awesome time to draw closer to God and learn to depend and trust Him more.

Since there is **no failure in God**, we cannot choose to fail at anything as an option. We can be successful because God will give us the strength; just have faith and believe that He will not fail us, but will make it happen in our lives.

"I have declared my ways, and thou heardest me: teach me thy statutes. Make me to understand the way of thy precepts: so shall I talk of thy wondrous work. My soul melteth for heaviness: strengthen thou me according unto thy word" (Psalms 119:26-28).

19 July ~ "The Signs of My Return"

As I prepare to return home, I've already sent my first foot locker containing gifts and clothes and items I don't need here. Receiving my foot locker will be the first sign Frank will receive that I'm on my way home!

Similarly, Jesus has given us **signs of His return** to retrieve us from this old world into a new heavenly home! These signs are written in Matthew 24; which speaks of *"wars and rumors of wars"* (Syria issues are now brewing), and *"earthquakes in diverse places"* (we just had another one a week ago; having them in Maryland and DC are unheard of, but we experienced them last year).

These are the signs that time is drawing nearer. Get ready people of God, for the **signs of His return** are clear and imminent!

"And there shall be signs in the sun, and in the moon, and in the stars; and upon the earth distress of nations, with perplexity; the sea and the waves roaring; Men's hearts failing them for fear, and for looking after those things which are coming on the earth: for the powers of heaven shall be shaken. And then shall they see the Son of man coming in a cloud with power and great glory. And when these things begin to come to pass, then look up, and lift up your heads; for your redemption draweth nigh" (Luke 21:25-28).

19 July ~ "Yes is the Answer: What's the Question?"

I had a teachable moment during a briefing by the Policy, Strategy, Partnering and Capabilities Commander. The comment he made just blew me away! **"Yes is the answer, what's your question?"** He wanted us to know that he was flexible, amenable, and ready to assist us with our needs. Just ask, and he would find a way to say yes and get it done—what an awesome way to lead.

God is always there to answer you. You just need to seek Him and ask the question. He is willing and just according to the plan for your life, to give you the desires of your heart. If you want more wisdom, ask!

"Ask, and it shall be given you; seek, and ye shall find; knock, and it shall be opened unto you:" (Matthew 7:7).

19 July ~ "Dig Deep Down to the Roots"

I was watching the contract workers dig, pull, and chop at weeds and stumps growing at one of our sites. They used a sickle, then a shovel to dig deep down under the roots to get rid of the weeds.

Of course, this is the old, primitive way of rooting out weeds and stumps.

In order to root out the sin in our lives, we must go **deep down**

to the root of our issues or problems, especially with the sin that so easily overwhelms us. Then, we can pour weed killer (the Holy Spirit) on the affected area to keep it from growing back again! We want to ensure that we purge the old stuff away, so we can produce the fruit of the Spirit.

Let the Word of God richly dwell in your hearts as you study and obey God's Word.

"He spake also this parable; A certain [man] had a fig tree planted in his vineyard; and he came and sought fruit thereon, and found none. Then said he unto the dresser of his vineyard, Behold, these three years I come seeking fruit on this fig tree, and find none: cut it down; why cumbereth it the ground? And he answering said unto him, Lord, let it alone this year also, till I shall dig about it, and dung it: And if it bear fruit, well: and if not, then after that thou shalt cut it down" (Luke 13:6-9).

20 July ~ "Kill Him with Kindness"

Today I had a meeting with my Senior Logistician (who is extremely cantankerous), my Commander, and the HQ Chief. We discussed the challenges we were having with logistics and how we could resolve the issues. Previously, I spent time with the Senior Logistician to warm him up to becoming a team player and to be gentler when responding to the staff.

At the end of the video conference, I gave the Senior Logistician a big hug, which shocked both him and the HQ Chief. They all laughed and agreed that we were getting along much better. I took the opportunity to express my desire for us to work together in a cohesive manner to ensure we met the mission requirements.

I learned that I can put aside the fear of revolt and rejection and be led by the Spirit to engage someone who may not be agreeable. I was determined to show love and not censure him.

"Judge not, and ye shall not be judged: condemn not, and ye shall not be condemned: forgive, and ye shall be forgiven:" (Luke 6:37).

21 July ~ "By Name Request"

As I thought about my new job and how I didn't even have to apply for it, my former boss said he **requested me by name** to the Deputy Director to work for him. This **by name request** was due to his knowledge of my excellent contributions in assisting with the establishment of another office in 2006.

Paul called for Timothy **by name** to help him in the ministry. Even though Paul had issues with Timothy early on, he knew that God had His hands on the young man and his ministry. He knew Timothy had grown and matured in the gospel and would be a perfect asset to the up-building of the Kingdom of God.

Jesus will provide the pathway to God every time with no questions asked. His **name** is our access to heaven.

"But I trust in the Lord Jesus to send Timotheus shortly to you, that I also may be of good comfort, when I know your state. For I have no man likeminded, who will naturally care for your state. For all seek their own, not the things which are Jesus Christ's. But you know the proof of him, that, as a son with the father, he hath served with me in the gospel. Him therefore I hope to send presently, so soon as I shall see how it will go with me. But I trust in the Lord that I also myself shall come shortly" (Philippians 2:19-24).

22 July ~ "Capture What You'd Like to Freeze"

While in a senior video conference session, the screen froze. It was interesting to see the gestures of the different people on the screen. Gestures frozen in time; some good, funny, and bad.

There are spiritual moments we'd like to freeze and enjoy forever, like worship, praise, and the entrance into the holy of holies. These are moments in our lives that we'd like to capture—Kodak moments to cherish forever.

Think about a moment you'd like to **capture and freeze** forever!

"I remember the days of old; I meditate on all thy works; I muse on the work of thy hands" (Psalm 143:5).

22 July ~ "Look Up"

I was gazing up again today. As I looked at the clear blue sky, it was radiant with the sun, and so serene. At night, the stars were so vivid that they looked close enough as to be able to reach out and touch them. With all the turmoil down here on Earth, a look at the heavens gives us a sense of peace and tranquility. God gave this to me as I was gazing.

No matter where you are in the world, **look up** and you'll see heaven!

"And lest thou lift up thine eyes unto heaven, and when thou seest the sun, and the moon, and the stars, even all the host of heaven, shouldest be driven to worship them, and serve them, which the LORD thy God hath divided unto all nations under the whole heaven" (Deuteronomy 4:19).

23 July ~ "The Enemy at Work"

I received some bad news today regarding one of my mechanic contractors. He committed a security violation. It wasn't intentional, and so my heart sank when I was told the incident may cost him his job. The enemy of my soul has been on my back, trying to discourage me. Losing staff that really worked hard for me was difficult. Potentially losing another is devastating.

I had a thought—the enemy is working everywhere to ruin the lives of the workers who ran this place flawlessly. The contractors that I depended on to make this place run efficiently were under attack. The **enemy was working** on my confidence in my ability to succeed. The enemy is doing this to get me down. I prayed for God's strength and deliverance. "Lord, you know I can't do this without telling someone off. Please take care of the situation. My heart is really heavy right now. My prayer is for the contractor to retain his job and get through the security review."

God answered my prayer. We completed the paperwork and the investigation resulted in the contractor being reprimanded, but kept his job. "Thank you Lord! You are greater than any circumstance and I choose to believe Your report. Too bad, **ENEMY** of my soul. Even though you're **always at work**, God has everything under His control!"

"I had fainted, unless I had believed to see the goodness of the LORD in the land of the living. Wait on the LORD: be of good courage, and he shall strengthen thine heart: wait, I say, on the LORD" (Psalms 27:13-14).

24 July ~ "This is Not a Bad Place"

I am enjoying another beautiful day in Afghanistan. I took a moment to rest in the lounge chair in the shade, enjoying the sun, warmth, and slight breeze. This was my silent prayer: "God, You are awesome! I still can't believe I had this opportunity to come here; it was only through Your grace and mercy that I did.

Lord, I pray for the people of Afghanistan and their land. I pray for peace and prosperity. I have purchased items to contribute to their economy because I see people working hard every day, trying to make a living. I've come to realize that **this is not a bad place.** It is the leaders who are corrupt and destroying their own people and their own land.

Lord, please change the hearts of men and help them to learn and know of You, the only true and wise God. Help those who kill, steal, and destroy realize they are wrong and there will be consequences for their actions.

Lord, I don't know the linkage between the Afghans and biblical times, but You are not willing that any man should perish, but receive Your Son Jesus by departing from their wickedness. I know there are people in this land that know You and serve You."

"Righteousness exalteth a nation: but sin is a reproach to any people" (Proverbs 14:34).

25 July ~ "Represent"

This was a very special day! I was able to share the love of God and Jesus to a 19-year-old Afghan contractor. He stated that I was the first American that he'd had the opportunity to talk to. He said I **represented** America very well. I asked him about his fasting and how he was doing. This is Ramadan season where the Muslims fast for 30 days.

During their fast, they do as we do in going without food and water all day. They also pray for spiritual renewal. We talked about it, and I shared that God's love for all of us extends across the world. I vowed that I would pray for the people and land of Afghanistan, that they would know the blessings of God. It was a blessed occasion for me because I've prayed for the opportunity to share Jesus with someone from Afghanistan. I'm not sure if he understood, but I believe that, through my witness, God will draw him and water the seed I planted today.

The teachable moment from this engagement was "**represent**." We, as children of God, should **represent** the cross in such a way that people are in awe of God. This young man felt comfortable enough to say that I was a blessed mother like his mother and that he would pray for me and my family during his fast. He noticed that I was different from what he was told about Americans. He said, "Oh, there are good people in America." We want the same said about God's people. Even though some Christians do not **represent** their faith as they should, there are those who God has placed as special anointed ambassadors to **represent** Him.

My prayer is that I have **represented** God to the young man in a way that he could understand and thirst for more. He's a good kid and has educational goals to help his family and country. He thanked me for contributing to their local economy.

His name is Fawad. He is 19 years old and has seven brothers and three sisters. There are 13 people living in their house. He plans to graduate and enroll in Kabul University. Please put him on your prayer list!

"And this gospel of the kingdom shall be preached in all the world for a witness unto all nations; and then shall the end come" (Matthew 24:14).

"And he said unto them, Go ye into all the world, and preach the gospel to every creature" (Mark 16:15).

26 July ~ "I Gave Away My Helmet?"

Today **I gave away my helmet**. Why would someone do that in a combat zone?

I loaned my helmet to a technician who needed it in order to travel on a military flight. So how do I protect myself if I need it? *Great question!* Keep my head low and out of the line of fire and stay clear of areas where my head could be hit.

I did contemplate not giving it up, but I wanted the mission to be completed. It was his fault for not getting a helmet while he was in Bagram. I decided to trust God that I would not need it during the four days that he would be on travel. I put my own safety in jeopardy for someone else and the mission. Not that we were in any imminent danger, but it is part of our battle attire and should be with us at all times when off the Compound.

There may come a time when you may have to put yourself in harm's way that others might live. That's laying down your life for someone else, and demonstrates *agape* love. I had complete faith in God after I made the decision to give the helmet away that the Lord would be my helmet and protector if needed. Actually, I had trusted in God before making the decision—if I didn't, I would not have given it up!

"For scarcely for a righteous man will one die: yet peradventure for a good man some would even dare to die" (Romans 5:7).

"For God so loved the world that he gave his only begotten Son, that whosoever believeth in him should not perish, but have everlasting life" (John 3:16).

27 July ~ "Respect the Position"

Following my Tallit Prayer time, I was thinking about how God had protected me while overseeing the Afghan contractors who are all males. Some look at me like I'm a weirdo and some with amazement that I am a woman in a position of authority.

Some don't know what to say to me or if they should even talk to me. It is their culture not to approach a woman. Also, in this culture, women are not regarded as someone who should be in authority. With these workers, I have never projected myself to be better than they or authoritative.

I am just an official who was there to oversee their work, get them water, and get them badged in and out of the Compound. They must ask me for permission to go the porta potty, get water, and leave the site. They all use "ma'am" when addressing me. I feel so unworthy and humbled to even be in a position where I'm regarded with such respect and authority.

The 19-year-old, Fawad, was part of this group of Afghan workers. He said I was different, yet an excellent example of an American. When God places us in a position of authority, He sets us up for a purpose to give Him glory and honor. We should feel honored to be used by God to act on His behalf in advancing the kingdom.

We are to serve the poor and needy and be hospitable to those we meet. We must respect the positions of authority of those whom God has placed over us, for they watch for our souls. We must learn that God has put them in the position they are in for His glory. We can't interfere with God's plan. Having authority is an incredible position to be in. We must take on that role with prayer and humility. An overbearing dictator is hated by the followers.

Teachable moment: when you are placed in a position of authority, immediately humble yourself and stay grounded so you don't get high-minded. **Respect the position** before you perform in that position.

"And when Jesus was entered into Capernaum, there came unto him a centurion, beseeching him, And saying, Lord, my servant lieth at home sick of the palsy, grievously tormented. And Jesus saith unto him, I will come and heal him. The centurion answered and said, Lord, I am not worthy that thou

shouldest come under my roof: but speak the word only, and my servant shall be healed. For I am a man under authority, having soldiers under me: and I say to this man, Go, and he goeth; and to another, Come, and he cometh; and to my servant, Do this, and he doeth it. When Jesus heard it, he marvelled, and said to them that followed, Verily I say unto you, I have not found so great faith, no, not in Israel. And Jesus said unto the centurion, Go thy way; and as thou hast believed, so be it done unto thee. And his servant was healed in the selfsame hour" (Matthew 8:5-10, 13).

27 July ~ "The Smiling Faces"

I had to get up at 0300 hours to get to the internet kiosk in order to video conference with Bruce Thornton (our church's Chief Sound Technician) during our Gospel Spreading Church 2012 Convocation. I made earlier arrangements with Bruce to connect me on the big screen so I could greet the church members attending our bi-annual Convocation. I wanted to surprise Frank, my husband, who would be in attendance.

The bandwidth was slow and the video choppy, but I did get to see **the smiling faces** of the saints back home and my dear husband Frank, who was overtaken with emotion. I gave my testimony and had a chance to see some of the people in the room. It was a great feeling and powerful motivator. It reminded me of a runner in the race who gets that extra push from family and friends on the sidelines—it provided me the extra strength to finish my race.

"But charge Joshua, and encourage him, and strengthen him: for he shall go over before this people, and he shall cause them to inherit the land which thou shalt see" (Deuteronomy 3:28).

28 July ~ "Depart From Me, I Know You Not!"

As the Executive Officer (XO), I directed that four of our men be taken to sick call at the other Compound: the Commander, our electrician (who was a contractor), and our two senior officers. One officer had been sick for weeks. He lost 10 pounds and we were all concerned about his health. Each one experienced weakness, tiredness, and gastrointestinal issues. All had partaken of food in our dining facility that made them sick. The doctors treated all but one, the contractor. Contractors cannot receive medical treatment at this facility. The others received CIPRO (ciprofloxacin) to help kill the parasite. We got some CIPRO for the contractor through another provider. The fact that the military medical facility did not recognize the medical needs of the contractor due to his **status** really bothered me.

I thought about the scripture where sinners will be denied heaven **status** as God will not acknowledge them. This also bothers me, not that I think God's plan is unfair, but that people won't learn from past experiences and continue to be blind to righteousness. Like God, I am not willing or happy that anyone should perish. We can do a lot of good in this life but if we don't have a relationship **status** with God, we're working in vain. It is not by the works that we do, but by the faith that we have that God sent His Son to die on the cross for our sins. And, if we believe, we shall have eternal life.

"Many will say to me in that day, Lord, Lord, have we not prophesied in thy name? And in thy name have cast out devils? And in thy name done many wonderful works? And then will I profess unto them, I never knew you: depart from me, ye that work iniquity" (Matthew 7:22-23).

29 July ~ "Loyalty in Question"

Today I learned of a potential issue with one of our Afghan guards. The guard was mad with the Guard Commander for various reasons. This guard, who was leading this revolt against the Commander, once questioned the Commander about interceding for two of our team members one night. The Afghan Police (AP) had stopped them and one was ready to shoot them—this schemer told the AP that they could do what they wanted to do with them.

This situation put us in question as to the **loyalty** of these guards to do their job to protect us. It is scary to think of it with all the "green on blue" attacks by members of the AP and army against coalition forces we've had within the last six months.

My prayer: "When questioned or my faith tested, will I stand the test of **loyalty** to Christ? Do I really care about the mission and responsibilities to the point of fulfilling them at any cost? God, help me to think of the cross and its significance to my salvation.

Lord, when expected to fulfill my Christian duties; let me be led by the Holy Spirit. Let not my **loyalty** to You be questioned!"

For true believers, **loyalty** is shown in our commitment to Jesus and His gospel.

"And when he had called the people unto him with his disciples also, he said unto them, Whosoever will come after me, let him deny himself, and take up his cross, and follow me. For whosoever will save his life shall lose it; but whosoever shall lose his life for my sake and the gospel's, the same shall save it" (Mark 8: 34-35).

30 July ~ "Get It When You See It"

I accompanied our new Facility Engineer to our other Compound to get some items from the PX (Post Exchange). He was in there so long that, when he came out, I told him that he shopped like a woman! He stated that he was trying to find the pink lotion hair moisturizer. He said when he was here before, they had plenty on the shelves. But today, when he needed it, they had none! I told him that he should always **get it when he sees it**.

It has happened to me before. It was that still, small voice that said, "You should get this now because it may not be here later." Well, due to hurry or doubting that the item will be gone, I shrugged it off and thought I would get it another time. But often I was highly disappointed when I went back and it was not there.

There will come a day that the Word of God will not be able to be openly preached like it is now. We had better get it while we can! We may end up in a place or a foreign country where it will not be available when we want to hear something from the Word that will strengthen and sustain us.

Don't procrastinate; read, study and absorb the Word of God while it is readily available. Get your oil and fill your barrels—you'll need it later. Trust me, you'll need it in the by and by.

"Seek ye the LORD while he may be found, call ye upon him while he is near" (Isaiah 55:6).

31 July ~ "Heading Home"

The word **"heading"** is a current action, not in the past. I'm packing up, getting ready, getting ready to go! I'm **heading home!**

Spiritually, we're packing daily as we head to our eternal home—heaven! There's preparation required in which we ready our souls for the journey. The ticket of salvation assures us access to His glorious kingdom. Packing is exciting, but it can be stressful. We'll have stressful moments on this side and these can cause discouragement, but we should hold our heads up high because the journey will be rewarding once you get to your destination. I'll be glad to see HOME! I will also be delighted to see JESUS when that day comes!

"And I saw a new heaven and a new earth: for the first heaven and the first earth were passed away; and there was no more sea. And I John saw the holy city, New Jerusalem, coming down from God out of heaven, prepared as a bride adorned for her husband. And I heard a great voice out of heaven saying, Behold, the tabernacle of God is with men, and he will dwell with them, and they shall be his people, and God himself shall be with them, and be their God" (Revelation 21:1-3).

AUGUST 2012

1 August ~ "Count Down"

Today my learning was focused again on packing. You just can't take everything with you! As I **count down** the days to finally leaving this place and going home, I have a bag of mixed emotions. I'm sad to leave and happy to be going home.

I have marked each day on the wall calendar in my room and at my office desk to visually see the number of days accomplished and the number of days yet to reach before I begin to transition back home. I cleaned out the closets and drawers so that I would know just how much stuff I could pack in the foot lockers.

As we experience the countdown to the return of Christ, we must realize that we will not need to take any baggage with us. We need to lose the weight that can hold us down and remove those items from our temples.

"But godliness with contentment is great gain. For we brought nothing into this world, and it is certain we can carry nothing out." (1 Timothy 6:6-7).

2 August ~ "A Story You Can Believe"

Who said the weather and air quality would be awful here in Afghanistan? It has been great! You can't believe everything people tell you.

Colleagues gave me so many stories prior to my deployment—some really hard to believe. I got tons of advice from different people, some good and useful, others were way off track.

Here's an absolutely verifiable story. The story is of Jesus, how He came into the world as a babe, lived and walked among the people, healed the sick and gave sight to the blind, was crucified and died on the cross for the sins of the world, rose from the grave on the third day, was seen by many following His resurrection, and ascended into heaven to be with His Father—God Almighty!

Now that's **a story you can believe**! There were so many witnesses, but they all had the same story line. Keep on believing the miraculous story; it will come alive in your life once you accept it to be true.

"And the angel said unto her, Fear not, Mary: for thou hast found favour with God. And, behold, thou shalt conceive in thy womb, and bring forth a son, and shalt call his name JESUS. Then said Mary unto the angel, how shall this be, seeing I know not a man? And the angel answered and said unto her, The Holy Ghost shall come upon thee, and the power of the Highest shall overshadow thee: therefore also that holy thing which shall be born of thee shall be called the Son of God. And, behold, thy cousin Elisabeth, she hath also conceived a son in her old age: and this is the sixth month with her, who was called barren. For with God nothing shall be impossible. And Mary said, Behold the handmaid of the Lord; be it unto me according to thy word. And the angel departed from her" (Luke 1:30-31, 34-38).

3 August ~ "Unfinished Business"

As I prepare to depart, I'm thinking of unfinished projects and tasks. God gave me enough time, but other priorities prevented me from achieving every goal and every task. It was my goal to get SharePoint on the network and workstations as well as renumber the rooms.

But most of all, it was my goal to bring souls to Christ. I may never know whether I fully accomplished that goal. If someone that I touched gives their life to Christ later on, I probably won't ever know about it, but it is really not important for me to know. I must TRUST GOD that His Word went forth and accomplished that which was intended. I have shared Christ with many while here.

Jesus, too, had some unfinished business after He was crucified and buried in the sepulcher. He got up from the grave and then appeared before many, including the women and disciples. Then, He ascended into heaven to be with God. But, He has **unfinished business**; He will come back for those indwelled with the Holy Spirit for our transition to Heaven. What a glorious day! I'm looking forward to that day when I stand before God and He says, *"Well done, good and faithful servant."* (Matthew 25:23.) At that point, all business will have been completed. Goal reached! Home Sweet Home!

"And one of the malefactors which were hanged railed on him, saying, If thou be Christ, save thyself and us. But the other answering rebuked him, saying, Dost not thou fear God, seeing thou art in the same condemnation? And we indeed justly; for we receive the due reward of our deeds: but this man hath done nothing amiss. And he said unto Jesus, Lord, remember me when thou comest into thy kingdom. And Jesus said unto him, Verily I say unto thee, Today shalt thou be with me in paradise" (Luke 23:39-43).

4 August ~ "Don't Get Your Fuel While the Truck is There"

I learned something new today from the incoming Executive Officer. He mentioned that you should not to get your gas when the fuel truck first comes to the gas station. He said they pump the fuel in the tank which is almost empty. There is dirt and sediments that have settled at the bottom of the tank. These things are harmful to your car's engine. So, I was informed that I should fuel up my car when the truck is NOT there.

When you come to the filling station, don't fill your spiritual tank while the truck full of naysayers, devourers, complainers is nearby. Instead, wait and let things settle down before you get in line for refueling. You don't need the debris of sin to infiltrate your spiritual tank. Contamination will occur and your spiritual man cannot perform the way it should. Let things settle down so that you get the good stuff from the top. **Don't get your fuel while the truck is there!**

🍎 *"Then said I unto them, Ye see the distress that we are in, how Jerusalem lieth waste, and the gates thereof are burned with fire: come, and let us build up the wall of Jerusalem, that we be no more a reproach. Then I told them of the hand of my God which was good upon me; as also the king's words that he had spoken unto me. And they said, Let us rise up and build. So they strengthened their hands for this good work. But when Sanballat the Horonite, and Tobiah the servant, the Ammonite, and Geshem the Arabian, heard it, they laughed us to scorn, and despised us, and said, what is this thing that ye do? will ye rebel against the king? Then answered I them, and said unto them, The God of heaven, he will prosper us; therefore we his servants will arise and build: but ye have no portion, nor right, nor memorial, in Jerusalem"* (Nehemiah 2:17-20).

5 August ~ "Lord Keep Me Day by Day"

Today I was thanking God for **keeping me each day**. This worship thought was ringing in my heart throughout the day. I considered the goodness of Jesus and all that He's done for me during my deployment. I thanked God for His divine protection and for the privilege of experiencing this incredible adventure. He has **kept me day by day**.

I accompanied the new Executive Officer (XO) to the International Security Assistance Force Compound in Kabul to introduce him to the XO for that forward support office. While there, I took a picture in front of Florence Village. It was exciting to see a housing location with my name on it. VIPs often used these quarters including General David Petraeus. God kept me safe so I could see this village and take a snapshot prior to my departure.

It has been a day-by-day faith walk. Each day had its challenges that gave me opportunity to look to Him for wisdom and counsel. He also sustained me when I missed those at home and thought about how He added no sorrows to my days.

"The blessing of the LORD, it maketh rich, and He added no sorrow with it" (Proverbs 10:22).

6 August ~ "The Imminent Threat"

Once again, I thank God for His divine protection as we traveled over the dangerous roadways in this country. I continue to pray and thank God for His shield around this Compound and His loving protection of all residents as we come and go.

Because we know and understand the ever-present risk outside the wire fence around the Compound, we are careful and never let our defense down. We cannot afford to become complacent and nonchalant. We are not unmindful that the enemy is ever seeking to kill, steal, and destroy lives and property.

The enemy of our souls is also working overtime to catch God's people off guard. There is a daily **imminent threat** we need to rebuke in the name of Jesus. We rely on God's intervention; this is when He confuses the enemy and foils his plans.

Those of us who are true believers know who is behind the calm and quiet that most of the country has experienced during my six months deployment and during the Muslim Ramadan season. The threat is ever present, but my God is all powerful and will always be everywhere, casting His arms around us to protect us from harm and danger. Who wouldn't serve a God like this?

God has not allowed me to have a spirit of fear. I fear not, because He who has made me will perform what He has purposed me to complete. I pray for God's strength to endure and finish my course. I must run home and tell somebody that Jesus can save and keep, even in Afghanistan!

Despite the **imminent threat**, people go about their daily duties; this frustrates the enemy. "God, You are awesome!"

"For God hath not given us the spirit of fear; but of power, and of love, and of a sound mind" (2 Timothy 1:7).

"Destroy , O Lord, and divide their tongues: for I have seen violence and strife in the city. Day and night they go about it upon the walls thereof: mischief also and sorrow are in the midst of it. Wickedness is in the midst thereof: deceit and guile depart not from her streets." (Psalms 55:9-11).

7 August ~ "Shine Through Your Clouds"

The sun is up early and shining so vividly—what's wrong with us? God gave us another day of life and more than a reasonable portion of health and strength. Stop complaining and get up and give God some praise, just like the sun!

The sun shines consistently and faithfully every day. Even when it rains, the sun is still shining. We just can't see it from Earth because of the rain clouds. Yet, if you go on a flight, you can see the sun shining above the level where it is raining.

When you go through your rainy and cloudy days, let the love of God keep you smiling and your light shining. We must understand that He is the creator of this Earth and all the elements sprinkled throughout the galaxy.   This thought and worship coincide with my learning today.

"And he shall be as the light of the morning, when the sun riseth, even a morning without clouds; as the tender grass springing out of the earth by clear shining after rain" (2 Samuel 23:4).

8 August ~ "While Waiting, Trust God"

I misplaced my phone charger and tore the room up looking for it. I prayed: "Lord, draw me near!" I was getting ready for our missions trip to the school and needed to charge my phone. I don't like to go off the Compound without a way of communications to text Frank. Plus, I wanted to take pictures of the event.

After listening to the still, small voice that said check next to wall and bed, I found it. God drew me to it! Prayer answered.

That's fine—it was a happy ending; but, how was my attitude during the waiting? I walked out of the room to the office trusting God that he would draw me to the charger well before departing the Compound. I remember how I felt, frustrated initially because I don't often lose my stuff!

I thank God for the peace while I waited.

"And therefore will the LORD wait, that he may be gracious unto you, and therefore will he be exalted, that he may have mercy upon you: for the LORD is a God of judgment: blessed are all they that wait for him" (Isaiah 30:18).

8 August ~ "The Heart of Giving"

Today we went to the Afghan Women's Education Center School in Kabul City to deliver the school and sports supplies for Afghan children. Frank assisted with collecting donations from the church members at home and sent 10 boxes of supplies to us for this mission. We packed them all in the TaliVan and we headed out in a convoy of four armored vehicles. We drove with only two vehicles together and the other two staged far enough behind to not look like a convoy. Convoys are often targets for the Insurgents.

The feeling of **giving** to those in need was so heartwarming and humbling. These kids knew nothing about backpacks. They didn't even know how to wear them. It was a joy to see their smiling faces light up when we gave them the backpacks filled with school supplies.

Thank you, Church of God, 4310 Edmondson Avenue in Maryland, for your kindness and love shown towards these children. I was so proud of my church!

"Defend the poor and fatherless: do justice to the afflicted and needy. Deliver the poor and needy: rid them out of the hand of the wicked" (Psalms 82:3-4).

9 August ~ "The House"

We conduct Hail and Farewells on a monthly basis because staff members are always coming and going. Below is my farewell speech to the staff.

The House

A house is just a house without the love to make it a home. When I signed up for this deployment, I was told that I was going to The HOUSE! Only after being here for six months, do I now understand why it is called The House!

A home is a place of refuge…safe and warm, free from the battlefield. Though residents come and go, this House is special; it receives everyone who comes to live here. There is no discrimination, nor unwelcoming signs hanging around. Everyone comes through the gates that swing on welcoming hinges.

I've been impressed with The House; it has everything I needed to make this my home for six months. To ensure that I would be comfortable, I brought 6 foot lockers and 1 duffle bag, all with items to ensure I had the comforts of home!

But, it wasn't just the things—open kitchen, lots of refreshments, snacks, 3 meals a day, basketball hoop, pool table, TV room, roof-top views of the mountains, laundry facilities, 2 gyms, ping pong table—it was the people who lived in The House who made me feel welcomed and accepted (as the first female XO). For that, I say THANK YOU! Thank you for allowing me to serve you as you are challenged daily to accomplish the mission of this platform.

I delivered a few words of gratitude to certain individuals and finally for the remaining staff:

Commander—for your leadership and support.

Hamed, Abid, Satar, Fazil, Hashmat—for the area familiarization tour of Kabul City, guidance and assistance during this tour.

First Sergeant—for your consistent drive to support the mission & delicious meals. I pray that no one else gets sick!

Pastor—for holding weekly Bible Study and Easter Sunday Service, and sponsoring the Afghan Women's Education Center mission.

Second Sergeant—for encouraging me to take on this challenge.

Sock Monkey—PLEASE COME FORWARD—for the support of, "Good Morning Florence" and the dagger in my back (with a SMILE).

New XO—take the bull by the horns and have at it! ENJOY!

House members—as I have prayed every day for the safe exits and returns for each of you—I ask that you continue to be vigilant and never become complacent—there is a true enemy outside these walls who desires to kill, steal and destroy lives and property. I leave you with this verse from the Scriptures: Romans 15:13—"Now the God of hope fill you with all joy and peace in believing, that you may abound in hope by the power of the Holy Spirit."

May God bless you all and be safe! Dugout, Dugout—this is Mother Hen…leaving her chicks in the nest to fend for themselves.

"Now the Lord of peace himself give you peace always by all means. The Lord be with you all" (2 Thessalonians 3:16).

9 August ~ "Enlarge My Faith"

I was thinking about how God has enlarged my territory as I have been blessed to be in a new place with new people with whom to share my faith. As I prayed, I thanked Him for also **enlarging my faith**! As the Spirit of God moved upon me in my daily walk, my faith in God increased to prepare me for the next day. The faith that God would preserve and protect me grew stronger as the months went by.

This enlargement request was not financial or physical. I wanted my faith in God to increase! God answered through the nights of Tallit prayers (thank you, Dr. Almeta Stokes for teaching me how to do this) listening, worshiping and writing; my **faith** and trust in God has been **enlarged**!

"And the apostles said unto the Lord, Increase our faith. And the Lord said, If ye had faith as a grain of mustard seed, ye might say unto this sycamine tree, Be thou plucked up by the root, and be thou planted in the sea; and it should obey you" (Luke 17:5-6).

"And Jabez called on the God of Israel, saying, Oh that thou wouldest bless me indeed, and enlarge my coast, and that thine hand might be with me, and that thou wouldest keep me from evil, that it may not grieve me! And God granted him that which he requested" (1 Chronicles 4:10).

9 August ~ "I Trust You"

The tables have turned. He worked for 24.5 years (sometimes two jobs) and **trusted** me with all his earnings to take care of our financial responsibilities. Now, I have **entrusted** him for the past six months with all my earnings to take care of our financial responsibilities. Yes, I must confess, I did check the bank account a few times to see where the money was going. But, I didn't interfere and I never questioned him. Now that's **TRUST**!

Not only has God joined us in loving holy matrimony, but He has sewn us together in **trust** so that there are no worries about faithfulness or concerns for one another. In **trusting** Frank, I was **trusting** God that Frank would be successful in managing the finances. That kind of **trust** is grounded with submission and respect. In God we both **trust**!

171

"The heart of her husband doth safely trust in her, so that he shall have no need of spoil. She will do him good and not evil all the days of her life" (Proverbs 31:11-12).

10 August ~"The Seller's Tale"

As my time here comes to a close, shopping is in order. I went to the Bazaar today to pick up a tailored Shalwar kameez, (Afghan men's attire) for Frank for $120. It was in support of the Afghan Women's Education Center. I think I have done well contributing to their economy. I did some window shopping at the other booths. These were the **sellers' tales**: "My friend, good price for you." "No cost to look; just stop in my shop and look." "Madam, I give you special price today."

I must acknowledge, I am not a haggler or a bargain shopper. I know that I have paid way too much for some items. I did okay on other purchases. Oh well, I was a contributor for someone to have food in their pot.

Satan also tempts us with luring words and phrases. I know he has tried some on you. "There's no harm in looking!" That's an old favorite and it gets the unbeliever every time. Don't be fooled by his devices and temptations. You can't window shop for evil things and expect to not be lured into sin. There is no haggling with the devil. Don't pay too much by heeding to the **seller's tales**. Be in tune to the Spirit of God and obey those words that bring life and assurance.

"For the wages of sin is death; but the gift of God is eternal life through Jesus Christ our Lord" (Romans 6:23).

11 August ~ "Empty Prayers"

Today we received a brief that, due to the approaching end of Ramadan season, some Muslims feel the need to be a martyr and kill Americans. Of course that put us on high alert and the travel restrictions went black (mission essential travel only).

The 15th is the "Night of Power" for the Muslims. They believe that they are doing something good in the sight of Allah. At night during Ramadan, I heard the neighbor Afghans praying and reciting the Koran accompanied by the sounds of singing. Their chants reminded me of the story in Daniel where the people prayed to their god who did not deliver them. But Daniel prayed three times a day, not for show, but because he wanted to worship and glorify God. He prayed to the only true and living God, the God who hears, answers, and delivers!

It is so sad to hear the people of this nation pouring out cries and prayers to Allah who doesn't hear or respond to their prayers. Their **prayers are empty**; they do not avail anything.

We must learn from others' experiences. We must have a thriving relationship with the true and living God if we want our prayers to be acknowledged and answered. No relationship equals **empty prayers**!

"And it came to pass, afore Isaiah was gone out into the middle court, that the word of the LORD came to him, saying, Turn again, and tell Hezekiah the captain of my people, Thus saith the LORD, the God of David thy father, I have heard thy prayer, I have seen thy tears: behold, I will heal thee: on the third day thou shalt go up unto the house of the LORD. And I will add unto thy days fifteen years; and I will deliver thee and this city out of the hand of the king of Assyria; and I will defend this city for mine own sake, and for my servant David's sake" (2 Kings 20:4-6).

11 August ~ "Satan, I'm Not Scared"

With the heightened alert and roads going black, Satan tried to put fear in my heart that I would not be able to leave on the 13th. The senior leadership on the Compound was fearful and did not want anyone to travel.

Satan, I'm not scared! "I've waited six months for this departure date and I will let nothing—I repeat, nothing keep me here beyond my assigned departure. You are a liar and the father of lies. What you fail to realize is that I trust God for a safe and on-time departure.

I'm outta here! **I'm not scared!**"

"…He [Satan] was a murderer from the beginning, and abode not in the truth, because there is no truth in him. When he speaketh a lie, he speaketh of his own: for he is a liar, and the father of it" (John 8:44b).

"Have not I commanded thee? Be strong and of a good courage; be not afraid, neither be thou dismayed: for the LORD thy God is with thee whithersoever thou goest" (Joshua 1:9).

"I sought the LORD, and he heard me, and delivered me from all my fears" (Psalms 34:4).

"The LORD is my light and my salvation; whom shall I fear? The LORD is the strength of my life; of whom shall I be afraid? When the wicked, even mine enemies and my foes, came upon me to eat up my flesh, they stumbled and fell. Though a host should encamp against me, my heart shall not fear: though war should rise against me, in this will I be confident" (Psalms 27:1-3).

12 August ~ "The Last Supper"

This morning, I sent my farewell email to the team and received an interesting response from the Commander. He stated that he wanted to incorporate into his daily life my concept of "teachable moments." He wants to practice learning something each day from his experiences.

"God, as you have taught me, so I will teach others how to stop and focus on what can be learned each day. May the life I live speak for me. May the light I shine speak of You!"

Later while at dinner, I told one of the Reports Officers that I was having my **"last supper."** We laughed because I was gloating for the past two weeks about going home because she still had two more months to go.

While packing, I thought about Jesus at His last supper and I had mixed emotions. I am sad to leave because I will miss all the new friends I acquired and I will miss "the house." I took a moment to think about what being here has meant to me for the past six months. A half-year has gone by and I spent that time away from Frank, the children, my family, my friends, and church family! Only God could give me the strength and courage to do that.

As my last night here in Kabul grows to a close, all I can say is "Thank You, Lord."

"For he that is mighty hath done to me great things; and holy is his name" (Luke 1:49).

13 August ~ "Don't Be Unnerved"

When I got to the office this morning, I learned that the roads were red—limited travel only. The Commander called me to his office to tell me that he couldn't face my husband and family if he let me travel to the airport and something happened. I thought he was joking, but he was serious. So I quickly got serious and put my foot down and told him I was leaving this Compound today. I told him my life was in God's hands and I would be okay.

It is rewarding when everyone around you doubts your situation but you decide to trust God and display confidence. God showed me today that what He had promised me He would deliver and on His time schedule. In life, we always want things to go our way on our time table, but patience and trust are required in order not to get unraveled when things don't happen as we planned.

The Commander reluctantly let me go. I got to the airport and the plane was delayed. There were no other flights leaving from Kabul to Bagram. I said to myself, "I'm stuck." I was on the edge of being **unnerved**. My driver and gunner left the airport and I wasn't able to reach them on the cell phone. Then we were told the plane had mechanical issues. I was no longer on edge; I had gone over the edge and really become **unnerved**! But God, who loves me so much, allowed for the plane to get repaired and on the way. At that moment, I didn't care about the mechanical issues, I just wanted to get on board and make the 45-minute flight!

I thank God for getting me out of Kabul safely in the midst of reports of attacks from the Insurgents. Even at my location, the report was not to travel due to the reported threats. "God, I trusted You to foil the plans of the enemy so that I could get home without incident. You are faithful!"

I arrived safely at Bagram. My next flight was scheduled to leave early in the morning for Qatar.

"Be careful for nothing; but in everything by prayer and supplication with thanksgiving let your requests be made known unto God. And the peace of God, which passeth all understanding, shall keep your hearts and minds through Christ Jesus" (Philippians 4:6-7).

"Heaviness in the heart of man maketh it stoop: but a good word maketh it glad" (Proverbs 12:25).

175

"Why art thou cast down, O my soul? and why art thou disquieted within me? hope in God: for I shall yet praise him, who is the health of my countenance, and my God" (Psalms 43:5).

14 August ~ "Patience is a Virtue"

I slept really well last night. I feel my body is requiring lots of rest and I am enjoying it. I got up and had breakfast with my room- and travel-mate. When our driver got us to the airport at 1200 hours for a 1500 hours flight, she was told that we were late and had to hurry to get our luggage palletized. So we rushed, only to sit and wait for an hour. Then, we were told to get a snack and come back. We did so and waited again for word of our flight departure. We waited, waited, then waited some more. I finally found a row of seats in a nearby waiting area and laid down to take another nap. I wanted my body and soul to rest in the Lord so I wouldn't get upset about something I could not control. I began to think about **patience being a virtue.** We finally left around 1920 hours, arriving at Doha, Qatar, at 2111 hours.

The waiting was hard, frustrating, and boring. I guess that's why Jesus told the disciples to occupy themselves until He comes. "Lord, give me the strength and wherewithal to wait, not only on You, but also during life's experiences and trials." Six months went by fairly quickly, but getting home seems to entail years of waiting. I thought about the scripture in Isaiah. "Thank You, God for those encouraging words."

God was really teaching me patience—again—as it was a virtue that I evidently lacked. But I found comfort in knowing that the wait wouldn't last forever and that I was on my way home!

"But they that wait upon the LORD shall renew their strength; they shall mount up with wings as eagles; they shall run, and not be weary; and they shall walk, and not faint" (Isaiah 40:31).

15 August ~ "Hell on Earth"

I was up early enough to turn in my government-issued Table of Allowances 50 (TA-50) gear and took a little time to explore the base. I did a little shopping at the Post Exchange and rode around the base on the shuttle bus. I had to use the latrine outside because the one inside the warehouse hotel was under construction. There was no air conditioning in these bathrooms, just a circulating fan blowing hot air. It was so hot that there wasn't any cold water in the faucets or toilets.

Not only is it 120 degrees outside, when the wind blows, it just blows hot air. I selected cold water for the finger washer last night but only hot water came out. I wondered when I showered why I couldn't get the temperature of the water to cool down. All the water on this base is hot!

The realization of **Hell** really hit home with me today. **Hell** is no joke! It will be hot, burning fire all the time no matter where you go. It makes me appreciate my air conditioned room which, by the way, is too cold.

When the rich man in **Hell** asked if Lazarus could put some water on his tongue, I could only imagine, based on my experience today, how he was feeling. There wasn't any cooling well in **Hell**. The water and the air are hot and the burning fire will be hot also!

Choose to be cool. It's cool to walk around with the latest gadgets and clothes but to *really* be cool, choose Jesus. Choose life everlasting where the cool rivers flow for your pleasure. **Hell is hot** and so is Qatar right now.

"And it came to pass, that the beggar died, and was carried by the angels into Abraham's bosom: the rich man also died, and was buried; And in hell he lift up his eyes, being in torments, and seeth Abraham afar off, and Lazarus in his bosom. And he cried and said, Father Abraham, have mercy on me, and send Lazarus that he may dip the tip of his finger in water, and cool my tongue; for I am tormented in this flame. But Abraham said, Son, remember that thou in thy lifetime receivedst thy good things, and likewise Lazarus evil things: but now he is comforted, and thou art tormented" (Luke 16:22-25).

16 August ~ "Excuse Me Lord, Is This Mine?"

When we got to the airport early to make the 0355 hours flight, I was in another zone, but asked the military airline attendant if I could select my seat. He told me no because my seat was already selected. I said to myself "Shucks, I want a window seat near the front." Well, the gentleman checked for me and said, "You're in row 24 and you have a window seat." I was thrilled with the window seat. It was a Boeing 747-400 double-decker! I prayed that he was right.

I got on the plane and had to do a double check on my seating. The leg room was enormous and I was in front of the wing. As folks in the south would say: "Shut the Front Door!"—I was in first class seating! Lord, I was going home in style. As I played with the gadgets on the seat, which laid back and extended the foot rest forward, I marveled.

Then I heard a young soldier speak to the stewardess to make sure he had the right seat (next to mine), **"Excuse me, but is this my seat?"** She said, "It sure is." He said, "WOW, I'll take it!" She said, "You'd better!" Clearly this dude had never flown first class before. He checked out all the gadgets, took his pillow and blanket and wrapped up, pushed his seat back with the footrest in position, ready for the trip. Only, he didn't know that he had to push his seat up for the take off! I thought, "No, I won't tell him—I'll let the stewardess tell him." Then, I did the right thing and told him. He was thankful.

And I did the same thing this young soldier did, checking my boarding pass three times and playing with the gadgets. YES! God, I asked for a window seat ahead of the wing and You gave me that and more—first class, leg room, reclining seat with video and massage. Who wouldn't serve a God like this? **Excuse me Lord, is this mine?**

The teachable moment was when God blesses us with something out of the norm, we are so amazed that we don't believe it possibly can be ours! He's just that kind of God, always looking out for us, providing us with the best, like the giving of His only begotten Son. He did that just for me! I'm so undeserving of all the blessings; that is why I stay humbled, because I know it didn't have to be that way. He's an awesome, loving, and caring God. He wants the best for His children.

I arrived at BWI Airport at 1720 hours on American soil— "Thank You, Lord!" My family and church friends were there to greet me with balloons, flowers, and a banner. I really felt like I had a hero's welcome. But, I'm no hero...just a blessed child of God. I am so grateful for my family, church family and friends who never ceased to pray for me—they prayed and God answered!

"For the LORD God is a sun and shield: the Lord will give grace and glory: no good thing will he withhold from them that walk uprightly" (Psalms 84:11).

CONCLUSION

Why Afghanistan? On occasion, God has to take you out of your comfort zone and send you to an unfamiliar place to allow you to experience a different culture and enter into a realm of His presence that is *extraordinary*. In hindsight, the story of Abram in Genesis 12 sheds light on my purpose and charge for this mission. I did not comprehend it prior to my deployment, but felt the urging in my spirit to submit and proceed. As a result of my submission, I have accepted His teachings and experienced the blessings of Abraham.

"Now the Lord had said unto Abram, Get thee out of thy country, and from thy kindred, and from thy father's house, unto a land that I will shew thee: And I will make of thee a great nation, and I will bless thee, and make thy name great; and thou shalt be a blessing: And I will bless them that bless thee, and curse him that curseth thee: and in thee shall all families of the earth be blessed" (Genesis 1-3).

As I reminisce of the events I experienced during my **179 (plus) days** of deployment, there is no way that I can go back to the same old life after being in the presence of God during my journey. I can only testify of His goodness, power, protection, and how I made it and didn't lose my mind or my life! I'm so glad I survived the experiences and finished my course!

There is nothing impossible with God. If He could do it for me, He can do it for you. Don't be afraid to step outside of your norm and walk on the waters of uncertainties. God will teach you how and allow you to walk in the *extraordinary* (as so eloquently given to me as a charge by my daughter, Christina, on 14 February 2012).

My initial scriptures were: Psalm 91 and Jeremiah 29:11. My completion scriptures were: Psalms 84:11 and Luke 1:49. Take time to look these up!

I pray earnestly that the words penned here will bless, motivate, and encourage you to yearn for a closer relationship with God. In that yearning, I entreat you to seek God daily for wisdom and understanding, that He will reveal through **teachable moments** His will for your life.

May God bless you!

Florence "Robyn" Smith

ABOUT THE AUTHOR

FLORENCE ROBYN SMITH is a self-motivated professional skilled in directing and orchestrating tasks to achieve overall project goals. She serves in many capacities within her church organization, Gospel Spreading Church of God, to include: Pastor's Armor Bearer, Head Deaconess, Organizer and Speaker for a quarterly Women's Power Hour, Bible Study Instructor, and Chairperson of the Publicity Committee for the Bishop's Work Team. She mentors the youth and young adults in her church and family, providing marriage counseling, parental guidance, and practical lessons learned. She has conducted speaking engagements at numerous women's gatherings, church graduation programs, and special church services.

Florence has been employed with the Department of Defense since December 2004. She has held various management positions supporting some of the Nation's most sensitive activities; providing managerial and advisory support to members of the Senior Executive Service, Brigade Commanders, Senior Experts and General Counsels. She has received numerous awards to include civilian service awards, North Atlantic Treaty Organization Medal, Secretary of Defense Medal for the Global War on Terrorism, and Joint Meritorious Unit Award. She is a member of the National Association of Professional Women, Federally Employed Women, and Christian Small Publishers Association.

Florence has a Bachelors in Business Administration; Masters in Technology Management, both from University of Maryland University College; and will complete a Masters in Strategic Studies at the U.S. Army War College in June 2016.

A woman with a message of hope, encouragement, and inspiration, Florence will leave you motivated and enthused about fulfilling your purpose! Florence believes that inside of every person is boundless potential, and it is her passion to help them achieve their vocation.